3262

LATER DAYS

By
W · H · DAVIES

LATER DAYS

LONDON
JONATHAN CAPE LTD

FIRST PUBLISHED IN MDCCCCXXV
MADE & PRINTED IN GREAT BRITAIN
BY BUTLER & TANNER LTD
FROME AND
LONDON

Contents

7

LATER DAYS

LOVE kissed me in a strange, untruthful hour,
    All for a smiling lip and shining eye;
Not knowing that my thoughts were far from her,
    Set on a wonder in the years gone by.
It was the vision of a mighty rock
    That faced the East, across Long Island Sound;
From which a hundred tongues of water burst,
    And sang me into slumber on the ground.
And how I, waking in the night-time, saw
    A large, white butterfly of moonlight clinging
To that rock's forehead, while each silver tongue
    Shook faster than a lamb's tail, in its singing.

★

IT has been suggested that I should write a book
dealing with my life since I published my *Autobiography of a Super-tramp*. After some consideration I have decided that I have enough good
material to work on; and that the book can be written without the least suspicion that I am trying to
make common ditchwater sing like a pure spring.
Let us not judge life by its number of breaths,
but by the number of times that breath is held,
or lost, either under a deep emotion caused
by love, or when we stand before an object of
interest or beauty.

11

So, seeing that my life has been just as wonderful since I became known as an author as it was before, I will now make an attempt to impart some of that wonder to others. I will, therefore, go back to my early life in America, in case this book should fall into the hands of readers who know nothing of my past. It will also serve as a strange contrast, by introducing some of the immortals of vagrancy to the immortals of Literature and Art whom I have met in my later days.

Whoever walks the railroad in America will see, when he reaches the first wood outside a town or city, a small, well-beaten track. If the traveller is curious to know more, he will step off the railroad and pass under the trees. He will not go far into the wood before he comes to a fresh-water spring, at its very source; where it is seen as a large eye with tears running down the face of a dark rock — tears that come together again and make a small rivulet. After doing this, he will see a curious assortment of tin cans, in which men have made coffee. He will then know that he is in a beggars' camp. If he knows anything about beggars and the way they live, he will see by the position of the cans what kind of men were there last. If they were true travellers and professional beggars, the cans will be turned upside down, so that the dew or rain shall not get inside and rust them. For in his consideration for others, the true traveller is a gentleman. But if the cans are thrown about in every direction, lying on their sides, or with their mouths open to the upper air — if this is the case, it can be said with certainty that the camp was lately occupied by 'gay cats'; men who are only beggars occasionally, and not gentlemen.

One morning, in a wood on the outskirts of Baltimore, there was a notable gathering of professional beggars — Detroit Fatty, Saginaw Slim and Harlem Baldy were there, and others whose names were known through every state in the Union. Their names were carved on the water-tanks of their native country and on the trees where they had camped. It was another meeting of kings, and the wood was another Field of the Cloth of Gold.

At twelve o'clock, when the hooters were heard in the distance, to tell the business world to rest awhile for dinner, all these beggars looked at each other with meaning in their eyes, to show that it was dinner-time, and that the fact had not

13

escaped them. But these noble fellows, with the kind consideration of true travellers, were all of one accord in this — that business people, who had to work for a living, should not be begged until they had a chance to swallow a mouthful or two of their own dinner. For that reason it was ten minutes or more before these fine fellows left their camp and marched towards the city; and it was probably half an hour before they parted and scattered themselves into the various streets.

At three o'clock they had all returned to the camp, one after the other. They had all had hot meals, and were now to be seen taking various cold foods out of their pockets, for later meals, when they would make hot coffee. Their work was now done for the day, for it was summer-time, and the nights for sleeping out in the open air. Had it been winter, they would have worked a little harder and longer, being forced to beg the price of a bed in a lodging-house.

But these beggars had scarcely settled down for more than twenty minutes when it became obvious to them all that Detroit Fatty was not only unusually quiet, but was also in some strange distress. He was seen to bite his lip and to pass a hand over his forehead, and to glare defiantly at his companions. At last he could contain himself no longer and, turning to Harlem Baldy, shouted in a savage voice – 'What do you think of me?'

'What I think of you,' answered Baldy, with unconcern, 'is this: you are as fine a beggar as ever broke bread or breathed the breath of life. But I do not say this to flatter you. Allow me to say that, at the present time, you are playing the fool; and I would rather a man had nits in his head than foolish thoughts.'

But when Saginaw Slim spoke to Fatty in a more kindly voice, the poor fellow sat down on a fallen tree and rocked his head between his two hands.

Fatty's mysterious conduct soon affected the nerves of his companions, and it was not long before two or three voices demanded, as a right, to know what the trouble was.

'Boys,' began Fatty, rising to his feet and still speaking in a savage voice – 'Boys, what do you think of that?'

With these words he suddenly released his hands

from his coat-pocket and threw a small bar of soap into the centre of the camp.

'Boys,' continued Fatty, in a broken voice – 'Boys, I am no longer fit for your company, for I have now become a common thief. When I was leaving a certain house, I saw this small piece of soap on the window-sill and, forgetting that I was a well-known beggar, and not a petty thief – I stole it. Can you keep the secret, boys? Let my guilt not be seen in the eyes of my fellow-travellers, when I enter into strange camps. In stealing this bar of soap I have proved myself an unsuccessful beggar and false to my profession, and I have certainly won no glory as a thief. I, who could beg half a ton of soap in a day, to be guilty of stealing this!'

With these words the poor fellow kicked the bar of soap into the woods and then rushed out of the camp.

When Detroit Fatty had gone, there was much talk as to how so great a beggar could demean himself by stealing a common bar of soap. In the end, Harlem Baldy expressed it in these words – 'It was done, believe me, in a temporary fit of insanity.'

16

I have often wondered what became of Detroit Fatty after his disgrace. Would he be able to keep the secret to himself; or would he not, as soon as he had tasted strong drink, stop the first man or woman that came along, and, like the Ancient Mariner with his glittering eye, begin to tell his story? Would he cry out like a leper, when he passed an old friend — 'Do not touch me or speak, for I am not fit to be called a beggar. I am no more than a common thief.'

If Harlem Baldy is not right, when he said that Detroit Fatty stole in a temporary fit of insanity, what is the truth then? What strange fancy possessed his mind — the mind of a great and famous beggar — to make him steal a small bar of soap; a man who could have begged half a ton of soap in a day!

These are the scenes of my early days, when a literary life was only a dream that I saw no prospect of realizing. It was the days when I buried a shirt on the banks of the Mississippi. In that same year, on a midsummer's day, I buried a pair of boots near Cumberland, in the Alleghany Mountains; and then, before the leaves began to fall, I buried a coat under the rocks near Narragansett, on Long Island Sound.

When Posterity has confirmed this immortality which contemporary critics have conferred on me, I hope the British Government or private admirers of my work will fit out an expedition to go in search of those treasures and bring them back to my native land.

I will say no more than this at the present time, for we all know how eager and energetic the Americans are in matters of this kind ; and it must be remembered that these belongings of an English poet are all buried in American soil. But when I make my last will and testament, in a few years from now, I will also make a few charts to enable my countrymen to find the exact places.

These treasures were all buried in my early days, when I was tramping in the United States of America. The shirt was given to me by an honest, respectable woman, but it was too heavy for that time of the year; and for that reason I buried it safely in the earth, in case I should pass that way again and need it. Tramps in America often do this, and they never forget where their goods are buried, no more than dogs

18

forget where they have buried bones, or squirrels forget where they have buried their nuts.

But with regard to the shirt, I would like to give one word of warning, which might save valuable time, expense and trouble. The Mississippi is known to be a very erratic river, that is continually changing its course, and by this time the shirt has probably shifted. I don't say that the shirt has turned into a shift, which as a joke would be feeble indeed, but that it has moved away from its first burial-place. That being the case, my shirt is likely at any time to be found nearer home, hanging, perhaps, on one of our own beloved cliffs of Albion.

I am reminded again of thirty years ago when, still in America, I carried a most deadly punch everywhere I went – the very sight of me tamed everything except the wild landscape. Everybody knew, by the way I looked, and the way I walked, that I carried a punch that was to be feared and respected, and my rebuke would be dangerous indeed. When I went down the Iron Mountain Road into Tennessee, all the young buck negroes touched their caps and greeted me respectfully with – 'Good morning, Captain.' And the older negroes, being more servile, because they were freed slaves, made a reverent movement, as they half whispered – 'Good morning, Colonel.' One old negro, who, judging by his white hair and wrinkled skin, must have been a hundred years old, almost fell to the ground when he said – 'Good morning, General.' They all knew by my steady eyes, my lifted head and firm step, that I carried a deadly punch. The fact of the matter is this, I carried more than one punch – I carried six, and they were all deadly. I carried in my side-pocket the lives of six men – a revolver loaded in every chamber. The knowledge of having in my possession these six deadly punches gave me such a bold, proud look that no doubt every one suspected me of having them ready for instant use.

This went on for about three months, until I reached New Orleans; and it was on the outskirts of that old city that I not only lost my six punches, but almost lost my life as well. I was suddenly, without the least warning, attacked by several men. One of them struck me such a heavy blow on the side of the head that I heard birds singing in my ears immediately. Other blows followed in quick succession, and I was left there, to live or die. When I recovered my senses, my left eye was closed fast, and the other had a little light, about the size of a canary seed, to guide me on my way. I was so weak that the blood I lost would have probably made sufficient black-pudding to feed a small family. But what annoyed me most of all was the loss of my six deadly punches, which they had taken from me. However, I was soon asking myself this question — 'Why carry a punch, when other people will not give you either time or chance to use it?'

Strange to say, although I can still see the broken bridge of my nose, and a heavy, dark rim under my left eye, the result of those distant days when I carried a deadly punch, yet, for all that, my sight is not affected in the least. Although I wear glasses for reading, they are not absolutely necessary, for I often read my paper and forget to use my glasses. In fact, unless a man showed me a map of London drawn on the back of a stuffed flea, and wished me to notice particularly a sparrow on the dome of St. Paul's — if it were not for uncommon cases of this kind I would need no glasses at all.

It will be seen from the above remarks that what knowledge I have comes from real life and my own personal experience. What surprises me as much as anything else in life is that the more we read books and talk, the farther we get away from the truth. So, when a young lady proposes a journey by caravan through England, and suggests the romantic employment of a one-eyed driver, I, with my greater knowledge of real things, can say – 'No, no, no : a man with one eye can see too much.'

Again, when I read of a prizefighter who has a punch, I ask with surprise – 'What right has any man to step into the ring and call himself a prizefighter, if he has no punch?' A prizefighter without a punch is no more than cabbage without boiled beef, or a dish of beans without pork.

Time after time I am astonished at the mistakes men make who call themselves specialists. Why does the sporting man, in search for men to train into champion fighters, be so particular that they should be six feet or more in height, have straight bodies and straight eyes? Nobby George, with whom I crossed the Atlantic with four hundred head of cattle, and who was no more than five feet nine inches – Nobby George would have made skittles of those fine-looking giants. Why? Because he was not only awkward and ungainly, but was also left-handed. In addition to these advantages, Nobby George was cross-eyed. Where is the scientific fighter who can stand up before a left-handed man who is also cross-eyed? If you cannot catch his eye, how can you forestall his movements? Every side-step we make, to catch his eye, is only wasted breath. He appears to be looking elsewhere, and yet we know he is closely watching us all the time.

I knew Nobby George for a long time indeed, and only once have I seen anyone taking a liberty with him. It was when a youngster cattleman, who had a saucy tongue and smoked excessively, pointed at Nobby George and taunted him with these words:

'Georgie, Porgie, Pudding and Pie,
Kissed the girls and made them cry.'

Ten minutes after uttering these words, the youngster was struck by a bale of hay, which was being hoisted from the hold, and had to be attended to by the ship's doctor. Before the day was out, it was known all over the ship that a woman had been masquerading as a man, and would be detained in special quarters for the rest of the voyage.

These have been my experiences in the past, but when I come to write of my career as an author, I find that my struggles have not been very severe. I have not worn out the knees of many pairs of trousers in my attempt to climb Parnassus. It is not for me to say whether I have secured a small place on its many slopes – I will leave that to others. Sometimes I imagine myself exchanging winks with Posterity, who will be the final judge in this matter; but it is a very mysterious wink, and I cannot be altogether certain whether it is in my favour or not. One of my first admirers, dating back to 1906, still writes about me in this way – 'At one stride he reached the very front rank of living poets.'

Whenever I read this, in an unsigned article, and I have read it a good many times, I say to myself – 'There's my friend again, and still at the old game.'

However, in spite of reaching the front rank of living poets at one stride, I cannot say that it has brought me much worldly prosperity. In literature and art, as in other walks of life, this world seems to take a delight in stuffing fat pigs. But I have done the work that I have loved, and have had my reward in happiness. If I had said as many prayers as I have written poems, I would have probably been the Pope of Rome to-day, or at least a Bishop or Cardinal.

*

In my next chapter I will deal with my experience with literary men. My first book caused a little sensation, as much from the strangeness of my life as from any merit it might have. But Edward Thomas, who gave me a fine boom in several influential papers, knew that a poet could not live by poetry alone, and became a practical friend, finding me a small cottage in the Weald of Kent, where I was able to live on my small income of eight shillings a week, owing to my rent, coal and light being paid mysteriously by Thomas and his friends. Unfortunately, my second book of poems was something of a failure, because of my foolish haste to publish again, as is usual with new authors. So that I felt considerably disappointed when Edward Thomas began to tell me how so many authors sing themselves out in their first book, and then have no more to say. But when my second book was followed by *Nature Poems*, and my *Autobiography*, Thomas was then delighted to find that he had made a mistake.

The first poet I ever met was, I believe, Walter Delamare. This happened on one of the rare occasions I accompanied Edward Thomas on a day's visit to London. But as I am refusing to make this book a catalogue of well-known names, I am not to mention a great number of poets and society people whom I have met and parted from without anything particular happening. For instance, Delamare, as a number of people know, is a very charming man, but in thinking of him I am completely at a loss for copy. Every time I have met him, often at his own home, he has plied me with so many strange questions that I cannot remember anything we have been talking about. And when I get home and consult a dictionary about a word he has used in his questions, I find the definition to be even more confusing than the word, and impossible to apply to the question in hand.

On one occasion a man who had come to interview me asked me if I knew Delamare, and whether he was easy to approach, as he wanted to get him for his next interview. But although I said all I could in Delamare's favour, I certainly warned the man that he would come away as the interviewed and not the interviewer; that he would never interview Delamare, but that Delamare would interview *him*.

Up to the present time, I should think quite a hundred people have asked me if I knew Walter Delamare. And when I have answered 'Yes,' I don't believe there has ever been one case, whether the questioner was a man or a woman, where the question was not followed by these words — 'Isn't he a charming man.' But of the hundred people who have asked me if I knew Yeats, not one has discussed him as a man before they have said something about his work. No wonder a certain poet-editor ignored me altogether when I told him how difficult I found things because my pension, which at the time was only £50, was too small. 'How Walter Delamare can live and educate his children on less than two thousand a year is a mystery,' he said, ignoring my more modest claim altogether – 'and the Government should see that he gets it.' When a man's charm is so great that his friends say things like this, it seems to me that his life is dangerous, although he may be a fine writer, and he should be shut up for safety.

On one occasion Delamare asked me how I wrote my poems. This being a plain and simple question, I began in this way – 'First, an idea comes to me.' But I had no sooner said this than Delamare asked quickly – 'What do you mean by "an idea comes to you"?'

The reader will understand my confusion in trying to explain a thing that was so obvious.

Shall I mention the name of a well-known poet who was so modest, when he went to America, that the natives could not hear what he had to say – his voice was so quiet and low. But after three months of American hospitality and adulation, the natives could not hear his words for another reason – the voice had increased so much in volume.

There is another well-known poet who is so rich and well dressed that when I met him the other day in Charing Cross Road, I was afraid to speak to him for fear of being arrested for begging. And yet I knew him well and liked him too. I did not even dislike him when, not recognizing a friend and a fellow-poet, he held out his hand at Piccadilly Circus to prevent me from passing before his gorgeous car. But although this fine fellow is not very great as a poet, I have heard that when he entered a certain place in America, hundreds of the natives bared their heads in reverence. Why do the Americans think so much of our worst writers? It is very consoling to think that as soon as my power as a writer begins to fail in England, I shall begin a new life of greatness in America.

2: LITERARY MEN

WHEN I went down past Charing Cross,
    A plain and simple man was I;
I might have been no more than air,
    Unseen by any mortal eye.

But, Lord in Heaven, had I the power
    To show my inward spirit there,
Then what a pack of human hounds
    Had hunted me, to strip me bare.

A human pack, ten thousand strong,
    All in full cry to bring me down;
All greedy for my magic robe,
    All crazy for my burning crown.

★

WHEN I said at the beginning of this book
that my struggles as an author had not
been very severe, I did not mean the time before
the publication of my first book. I have already
told the public of those days, how I hawked
small articles through England to save enough
money to publish my first work. What I meant
was this — that my work was recognized at once
and, thanks to such kind-hearted and practical
men as Edward Thomas, Edward Garnett and

Bernard Shaw, I had no struggles worth speaking of. If I have failed at all, from a worldly point of view, it is entirely my own fault as a bad business man. For instance, I have always disliked sending my poems to the various magazines and, of course, that is where the money is. Again, when I published my first book the times were different from what they are now. When a young author publishes a first book in these days, we hear in a week or two that he accepts an important position on a paper or magazine. And in a year, or less, he is no longer regarded as a creative artist, but as a critic of other people's work. But although my first book caused something of a sensation, I am thankful to say that no job of any kind was ever offered to me. There was, I believe, some talk of getting me a small Government position ; but when Edward Thomas saw my face go white at this threat to my freedom, he communicated my disapproval to others, with the result that I was given a Civil List Pension instead. Perhaps I did not deserve it, but the British Government seemed to think so, seeing that it has been twice raised.

However, it is quite certain that my fame will

last. If I am not immortal as a poet, I shall be immortal as the greatest literary fraud of the twentieth century. As I believe that we have some kind of life beyond the grave, I have often imagined myself as a literary fraud in the regions of the dead and surrounded by questioning spirits. One will ask — 'How did you manage to deceive the public for so many years, that you were thought to be a good poet?'

Another spirit, who had been an artist in his day, will say: 'How did you manage to persuade the master artists of your day that you were a poet worthy of their attention?'

Another, a politician this time, will require an answer to this — 'How did you manage to get a pension twenty years before you were overtaken by old age?'

And when I have all these spirits seated comfortably around me, I will recite my verses — the verses that fooled the greatest people of my day. And what laughter there will be! Perhaps at that very moment we will be joined by another spirit, who has lately visited the earth, who will say to me — 'By the way, the *Westminster Bladder* has just mentioned your name. One of the critics has been warning a certain popular poet that he must not take himself too seriously, but remember the fate of W. H. Davies, whose work is now forgotten, and whose only title to fame is that he deceived for a number of years the greatest people of his day.'

None of the spirits will laugh more heartily than myself at hearing this. When I recite the lines at the beginning of this chapter, how amused they will be. But when I come to the last two lines –

> 'All greedy for my magic robe,
> All crazy for my burning crown.'

—when I come to this the hilarity will be so great that I shall not be heard when I say, 'This, Spirits of the Dead, is the kind of stuff that fooled the twentieth century.'

Now although I am going to write about some of the greatest artists and writers of their day, I feel certain that not one of them would take the least offence on hearing their names mentioned with the names of those other great artists – Harlem Baldy and Detroit Fatty. When we look into the woods, we see an old pair of boots, which have been so long emptied of feet, and so often wetted and dried by wind and sun, that they have become shapeless and gorgeous with mildew and moss. These boots have been discarded by Detroit Fatty, who has begged and gone off with another pair. Now suppose a wonderful still-life artist like William Nicholson came along and saw those boots, what would be the result? A beautiful picture that any of the best Galleries would be proud to hang on their walls. It is through my wide knowledge of different men that I am able to say this; and to express the deepest sorrow that Detroit Fatty's discarded boots never came under the eye of William Nicholson.

But my hand is now working faster than my brain, for I did not intend to write of artists first, who were my later friends, but of literary men. Artists and sculptors are not much interested in an author until they think he has established his reputation; and a young author must make the most of being photographed. For that reason my earliest friends were literary men, and the artists followed later.

It was at a restaurant in Soho that I had my

first meeting with literary men. I was taken there by Edward Thomas, and the presiding genius was Edward Garnett.

Garnett had organized these meetings for the midday meal on Tuesdays, and the regular attendants there were those who lived and worked in Town — Hudson, Garnett himself, Norman Douglas and a publisher's reader, whose name I now forget. But I cannot forget how facinating it was to watch that man's care and attention when removing the bones from a piece of fish, while his mind devoted the same particular care to the subject that was in hand. Other writers, such as Conrad, Edward Thomas, H. M. Tomlinson, Masefield, and sometimes an artist like Muirhead Bone, only came there occasionally, when they had come up from the country.

Hudson had his own gathering at his own house, on Tuesday evenings, but although he gave me several invitations, I never went to any of them, owing to there being no late trains to take me back home. On one occasion Hudson said I would meet a young Irishman there, called Robert Lynd, whom I have met since. As that young Irishman was not known in those days, it says a

36

lot for Hudson's discernment in making this special mention of his name, seeing that Robert Lynd has now become one of the most charming prose writers of his day.

Edward Garnett had a natural wit, and it had to come out, whether people liked it or not; but, being a kind-hearted man, he was very quick in smoothing matters over if he saw his words taken too seriously. On one occasion Stephen Reynolds came to lunch. It will be remembered that Stephen Reynolds lived with two fishermen down in Devonshire, and wrote several books dealing with their experience as fishermen, and their idea of other matters. But on this occasion Reynolds launched into a long account of Bob Wooley which bored everybody present, and Garnett had to head him off with the remark:– 'You live with two fishermen, but some day a man will live with *three* fishermen, and what will you do then?'

At this time Garnett had written a play called 'The Breaking Point,' which the Censor of Plays considered to be immoral, and condemned. But although the play lost the benefit of the Stage, Garnett was delighted to think that it would now have a larger reading public. Unfortunately for Garnett, the literary critics sent up a great cry that the play was a pure thing, without the least immorality. When this happened Garnett, of course, lost his reading public as well, for no one wanted to read a clean, pure work of literature.

My first meeting with Hudson was unfortunate indeed. It seemed to me that the idea of being old and unrecognized had embittered his mind. He was quoting Swinburne at the time, and when I said that I did not like Swinburne, he asked – 'Whom do you like then?' Not long after this he said, speaking of an author who had just received a certain honour, and whom he did not like – 'Well, he has his deserts at last;' using the same language as if the man had been a friend of his, but creating a different meaning by a bitterness in his voice. However, Hudson's manners improved when he knew me better, and he used all his influence in getting me a Civil List Pension.

It must be remembered that I have always been at a great disadvantage in meeting authors, for the simple reason that they knew my work and I did not know theirs. I do not know theirs because I hate the idea of borrowing books; and as I did not review literature for a living, as most of them did, I never got books for nothing. Two things must also be remembered: one, that I have never been able to afford to buy books by living authors, because of their high price. But I have been able to buy second-hand books of the great classics, some of which have only cost me a few pence. The other reason is that I go to Life and Nature for my own ideas, and have no need of books. However, I have a much better knowledge of the younger living writers, because some of them send me their work. But I have often told young authors, who have read my books, and then prove that they have no knowledge of the classics, that they are fools and training their minds the wrong way.

It will be seen from the above words that I had a great disadvantage in not knowing Hudson's works. My love of birds, which probably excelled his or any other man's, could not be made the subject of conversation, like his extraordinary knowledge of their life and habits. However, although I could not make much headway with Hudson as a literary man, he became quite interested when I told him about a tramp who could, with the help of a few sheets of paper, sleep in the open air in the dead of winter, and how it was done.

On one occasion I was warned by Edward Thomas that in going to the Mont Blanc Restaurant on Tuesdays I would meet a well-known writer whom I was certain to dislike. I was considerably surprised at hearing this, and wondered what kind of personality I would meet; for I had never in all my life taken a real dislike to anyone. My experience of life in strange places had taught me one good bit of philosophy, which was this – if I did not make myself liked, I must look for the fault in my own self, and not in others, and change my attitude towards them. Let me mention here, in dealing with my own personal looks, how much my face has inspired others with trust and confidence. In walking the streets of London so many strangers stop me to ask questions, that I often ask myself– 'Do they take me for a professional guide?' And when I mention that a number of these strangers are young girls that have just come up from the country, it can be said – 'How fortunate it is that a criminal mind is not at work behind that open face.'

But my face has passed a severer test than any of those – it is when I meet beggars, who never let me pass by without making an appeal for charity. This is the best thing to say in my favour, for beggars are without doubt – with the possible exception of gipsies – the best judges in the world of a human face. However, I do not set a great value on having this honest and good-natured face; for when I am out walking in search of green trees, I would rather not have my thoughts disturbed by strangers with their minds set on things of stone, such as St. Paul's and West-minster Abbey. Again, having this open and honest-looking face is nothing to my credit; for some of our greatest criminals must have had the same face, otherwise they would have been less successful in pursuing their evil ways.

It is not often that I have been abused or in-sulted, although I have spent a great part of my life in rough camps and low dens, not to mention my experiences on cattleships. One of my nearest approach to a fight was when I got into trouble with a London cabman. At that time I was cross-

ing the Thames Embankment near Charing
Cross and, being taken up with my own thoughts,
I walked in front of his horse, so that he had to
pull up sharply. When he called me a foul
epithet, I returned it with another, and it was
not long before we were abusing each other in
the worst language we could think of. Unfortunately for him, I had a large assortment of
Americans' oaths to add to my English ones, and
was soon getting the best of him. But we had not
been using this strong language for many minutes
when I suddenly felt a light pat on my shoulder,
followed by a sweet encouraging voice, which
said – 'That's right, little man, give him hell!
Give the flaming old swine double hell!'

When I heard that, my power of abuse failed
me at once, for I was not doing it for the amusement of others. The old cabman seemed to have
the same thought too, for he applied the whip
to his horse and drove away. So we both left
the young lady standing there, disappointed at
the sudden halt to a battle of words. It has only
been on one or two occasions of this kind that
I have ever got into trouble with other people.

We will now return to the Mont Blanc, where

I was to meet this man whom I was certain to dislike. I had arrived early on that occasion, and found our table — which was held in reserve — occupied by one man, who was a stranger to me. However, I knew that he would not be at that table unless he knew the party that used it on Tuesdays; so I sat down with the intention of waiting for some one to introduce us. But there was no need for this, for the stranger got up and introduced himself; and when I mentioned my own name he shook me warmly by the hand. In less than two minutes after this we were talking and talking with the greatest enthusiasm — talking of the joys of camping out in the open air. And this was the man that I had been warned of, that I was certain to dislike!

However, it was soon made clear that he was not so comfortable with other people as he had been with me. For after the others had come and were seated at their lunch, he scarcely spoke a word. Not only that, but he appeared to be trying to pack a lot of heavy matter into a few words, and lost the spontaneity of our first meeting. He became less genuine; he became, in fact, what he had been called — 'a dull fellow.'

43

But is not my experience with that man sufficient to prove that the fault was not in him, but in others?

Now although I am a rough man in some ways, yet, for all that, I have been called, more than once, 'one of Nature's gentlemen.' Which means, I suppose, that I am a gentle man. This being the case, I do not find it very difficult to get on with people, whether they are clever or not; whether they are rich or poor. If a person is a good talker, I am happy to sit and listen; and if a person has little to say, I make every effort to entertain him with my own voice, using it naturally, and not like an elocutionist or an auctioneer.

As I have said before, Hudson and I found it very difficult to converse. How he managed to read so many books and magazines I cannot say. Nothing seemed to escape him, and everything seemed to be read with a critical eye. This, of course, made him good company for such literary men as Garnett, Thomas, Norman Douglas and others, men who were doing a lot of journalism. But when I went to the Mont Blanc and found that Hudson had already arrived, he, knowing that it would be useless to ask my

44

opinion of certain books that had just been published, usually began to speak of the different
authors who were there the week before. 'Masefield was here last week,' he would say, or another.

One Tuesday, when Hudson was there alone,
and I was the next to follow, he said – 'You should
have been here last week.' He then began to tell
me how a certain author, who was closely connected with the Peerage, had stood in the middle
of the room and tried to balance a beer-bottle
on his nose. When I told Hudson that I thought
this action was quite natural in a man that was so
closely connected with the Peerage, he laughed.
And it took something to make Hudson laugh in
those days, when he was getting old and was
still without much recognition, and was worrying
over a sick wife.

A LONELY coast, where sea-gulls scream for
　　wrecks
　　That never come; its desolate sides
Last visited, a hundred years ago,
　　By one drowned man who wandered with
　　　　the tides;
There I went mad, and with those birds I
　　　　screamed,
　　Till, waking, found 'twas only what I
　　　　dreamed.

★

HUDSON used to enjoy these meetings at the
Mont Blanc and, not having any office ties,
like some of the others, was usually the first to
arrive. And as I was up from the country, and
had the whole morning to myself, it often happened that I was second. I may as well say here
that owing to being shy, this was deliberate on my
part. It saved me the ordeal of walking through a
crowded restaurant, and allowed me to be seated
in comfort before the arrival of many people.

By this time I had left my lodgings in the
country and had taken rooms in London, so
that I was now able to go to the Mont Blanc more
often. Strange to say, my coming to London was

not to meet people, but for more solitude. For I had become so well known in the little town where I had lived that I could not step outside the house without being engaged in conversation almost immediately. Not only that, but I thought that a change of surroundings would give me new thoughts, which it certainly did.

I have already said that Garnett had a most destructive mental punch, to which there was no answer. On one occasion we were joined by a young writer, who was only known to one or two of the party. But this young writer had no sooner given the waiter his order, than he opened a tremendous large manuscript and, to the astonishment of us all, began to read aloud. To make matters worse, his voice was high and squeaky, and soon became worse as he became more excited. However, Garnett's presence of mind soon came to the rescue; for he quickly seized on one of the passages and advised the young writer to alter it in a way he suggested. 'If you do this,' said Garnett, 'anyone will think it was written by Percival Gibbon or Stephen Reynolds,' who were there at the time, and who took it all in good part, although they knew that Garnett did not have a very enthusiastic opinion of them as writers.

Only once have I seen Garnett's words give pain, which he was very quick to remove. It was when some one asked Edward Thomas for his address. At that time Edward Thomas, being ill-paid for his work, had accepted several commissions to write books on different subjects, and these books were being announced by the different publishers. So when Garnett heard the question of Edward Thomas's address, he, thinking of all those books, answered quickly: 'Every publisher in London has it.' Thomas, who was overworked and in bad health, began to defend himself by asking how could he help it, was he not forced, etc. When Garnett heard this, and saw the effect of his words, it was not long before he smoothed things over, saying — 'Yes, yes, Thomas, we know that it can't be helped!'

This little incident was soon forgotten, for Thomas knew that Garnett was a good friend — a man who sometimes said hard things to your face, but always said soft things behind your back.

Some time after this I found, on reaching the Mont Blanc, that the room upstairs, where we usually met, was under repair and closed, and all customers had to use the ground floor. When I saw this I was on the point of leaving, but the proprietor came forward at once and motioned to a table half-way up the room, where I saw Hudson in possession, who was again the first to arrive.

I have said before that I am very shy. I am so shy that when I go to a party I seldom move from the first seat I occupy, until I leave for good, so as not to draw people's attention my way. But on this occasion there was no need of shyness for, when I looked into the restaurant, I saw at once that all the occupants of the various tables were smiling silently into each other's faces, and the waiters were walking about with bent heads, trying to keep their dignity. All this was due to one voice, one solitary voice in the whole place. So I had no sooner shaken hands with Hudson and seated myself, than I began to look around for a platform, or a man standing upright on the floor. When Hudson saw me looking around in this way, he said, 'That's Belloc; doesn't he talk!' This voice went on for over five minutes, and all we could do was to listen to it; for it was impossible for people to express their own thoughts, or even have thoughts to express. However, the voice stopped at last, and the room was soon full of other voices claiming their rights to use their own tongues. Belloc, I should think, must have forgotten where he was, thinking he was in the House of Commons or on a public platform. It was quite clear that the subject he was speaking about interested him deeply, or he would not have forgotten his surroundings.

When we were half-way through our lunch, Belloc left his table and came to ours, to ask Hudson to write an article for a new paper that he was starting. 'What do you pay?' asked Hudson, to my surprise. For at that time I thought authors left the question of payment entirely in the hands of an editor.

On hearing this Garnett, with his usual quickness to help a friend, said — 'You must have a lyric by W. H. Davies too.' Belloc took this as an introduction, and shook hands, saying, 'I didn't know you, pleased to meet you.'

However, I heard no more about the lyric, and thought perhaps that Belloc himself would contribute the poetry, especially to the first number. That being so, I must say honestly that the poetry would be in good and reliable hands.

On another occasion, Conrad, who happened to be in Town, came to the Mont Blanc to meet some of his old friends. But although his face lighted up when we were introduced, to show that my name was known to him, he simply made an expressive sign with his hands, saying something about not being able to talk to me there. From this I understood that he would have liked us to be alone together. When he left he made this idea certain by inviting me to pay him a few days' visit at any time I liked, and just to drop a line in advance to say that I was coming.

Some time after this, when it was near Whitsuntide, and I needed a breath of purer air, I remembered Conrad's invitation, and wrote to him. I judged that I would be less likely to interfere with his work if I went there at holiday-time. Back came an answer, by return of post, saying that he would expect me, and meet the train.

When I arrived Conrad was on the platform

waiting, and it was not long before we were shaking hands. But after this Conrad looked around, saying that he was also expecting a young countryman of his, who had come over on political matters relating to England's attitude towards Poland. It must be remembered that the Great War was now on, and every place was full of the movement of troops.

Hearing Conrad say this, I felt sorry that I had come, for I did not want to meet Conrad the politician, but Conrad the sailor and writer. And when Conrad and his young countryman began to complain that a certain sum to help Poland could not be raised, and yet England was doing all she could to help less deserving nations; when it came to this I began to feel uncomfortable, and did not know what answer to make. But although I nodded my head in agreement, I believe I said something about the English people being the most generous in the whole world; and that our papers were every day praising the gallantry of Scotch, Irish, Welsh and French troops, and saying very little about the achievements of their own.

That evening, when we all sat down to dinner,

Conrad and his young countryman talked in their native tongue, while Mrs. Conrad and myself at the other end of the table, had enough to say in English. In a few moments we had both found a subject to our liking, and had become so animated that Conrad forgot all about the troubles of Poland and asked once or twice — 'What are you saying?' On being told, he would smile approval, and would then return to the heavy, serious subject of their own. However, Mrs. Conrad was a charming woman, and full of ideas; and I felt that no conversation that I could have had with her husband would have pleased me more than the one I had with her.

On the following day I had Conrad to myself for an hour or more. His young countryman had complained of neuralgia, and was either resting in his room or had gone out for a walk. But I made a bad start indeed, as soon as we settled down to talk. Some time before this a man had told me that although Conrad had his Master's certificate and was a Captain, yet, for all that, he had never been in actual command of a ship, having retired from the sea before that time. As this man had asked me to put the question to Conrad, if I should ever meet him, I did so at once. But when Conrad heard this, he appeared to be quite upset, and offered to go upstairs for his papers to show me, and to mention the names of ships he had commanded. As soon as I saw Conrad's distress, I assured him at once that the man meant no harm by that question and that he was one of his greatest admirers. On hearing this Conrad appeared more pleased and satisfied.

Soon after we began to talk of our contemporaries, and Conrad began to question me about the work of a certain writer, saying that one of his prose books had been strongly recommended to him, but that after reading one chapter he had to give it up as impossible.

Just before this we had been talking of Civil List Pensions. So that when Conrad, with rather a worried face, asked me about that writer, I came to the conclusion that he had been asked to sign a petition to that effect. Conrad, I believe, wanted to be honest in the matter, but was troubled by an overkind heart. So when I praised the writer as a poet, Conrad smiled happily, and in a more settled mind – the petition was already signed. However, I may as well say here that the writer in question had so many influential friends, from the Prime Minister down through the most aristocratic ranks, that it would have made no difference at all whether Conrad had signed the petition or not.

The next thing, I believe, was to discuss the works of Masefield; not to discuss it as literary men, but as sailors. Conrad seemed to suggest that Masefield was not altogether true to life in his description of ships and sailors. On hearing this, I said that 'Dauber,' instead of being rejected and despised, would have been the most respected man on the ship; respected even by the captain and first officers, because of his unusual gift of being able to draw and paint pictures. I mentioned several cases of this kind, where the illiterate and poorest classes had respected a man of gifts, when he had accidentally been thrown into their own life. 'If the Dauber,' said I, 'was not respected by those honest seafaring men, it must not be put down to spite, disrespect, or jealousy of a gifted man, but because they disliked him for his personal conduct, or because they thought he was a sneak and carried tales to the captain. If that was the case,' I continued, 'he should have been made the villain, and not the hero of a story.'

Conrad agreed with all this, and said he had known cases of the same kind, where the life of a quiet dreamer like that would have been safer than any other life on the ship, or in the camp — wherever it might be.

These things, of course, had nothing at all to do with the poetical value of the 'Dauber,' or any other of Masefield's poems — we were only discussing their relation to real life; and both Conrad and myself were men who knew that life well, and had a perfect right to criticize any other man who should make it the subject of literature.

If anything equals my admiration of Masefield at his best, it is my admiration of him at his worst. At his worst he is extraordinarily good, as the following verses will prove —

> 'Her father struck
>   Jane on the head;
> Young Will upped
>   And shot him dead.

57

> 'Jane died soon:
> At high tide,
> At high noon –
> Jane died.'

I have a sincere and honest admiration for those two verses, for they are the two best bad verses that I have ever read. The flatness of that last verse is probably one of the finest things in English literature. Time after time have I tried to match those verses with lines of my own, and still I fail. Even the following sounds tame in comparison –

> 'Little boy,
> Big gun;
> Loud noise –
> Life done.'

So although I share the honour with Masefield of being included in the anthologies of the best poems, yet, for all that, I have a great fear that I shall never be able to write anything good enough to be included in an anthology of the best bad poems. I have such a dread of being left out of that book that I have made quite a number of efforts to match those two little verses of Masefield. Sometimes I think I have succeeded, as in the following lines from my opera, 'True Travellers.' It is about an old midwife called Martha, and is chanted by her great admirer Poll.

'Not all the revels, Martha, we have been to,
Can give us, when we're old, a peace like yours —
Due to the corpses you have gone and seen to.'

Although my readers may think this verse is not bad enough to be compared to Masefield's, I would still like to hear that I have made a good attempt. As I have said before, I am quite sincere and honest in saying this; for I do not bother my head much, or lecture the public on 'The Great Mission of Poets' ; and do not care whether I am called a poet or a rhymer.

Probably those two little verses of Masefield and the above lines of my own, have given me as much delight as anything else in Literature. They are to me a joy for ever, in the same way as the best passages in Shakespeare, Coleridge, and Keats.

When we were discussing other authors, I was rather taken by surprise to hear Conrad exclaim emphatically – 'Hudson is a giant!' I had never had the least idea that this was so, for, as I have said before, I had not read any of Hudson's books up till then. So hearing Conrad say this, I made a mental note of it, with the intention of reading something of Hudson's as soon as possible.

I may as well say here that in the course of a few days I got hold of a copy of *Green Mansions*, and found it one of the most fascinating books I had ever read. What a pity I had not known that extraordinary book at the time I was meeting its author! And why was I not told of it during the whole twelve months I was meeting Hudson, week by week?

But I was never to tell Hudson personally of my high opinion of his work, for the meetings at the Mont Blanc were now coming to an end. Owing to the illness of his wife, who had been an invalid for a long time, and who now did not like to have her meals alone – owing to this, Hudson was one of the first to be absent. Two or three others died, and then the coming of the Great War did the rest.

But although I was never able to tell Hudson personally how much I admired his work, I certainly was not backward in telling others; for I have sent many a reader to *Green Mansions*, and have never heard of a disappointment.

Strange to say, I was in the same position exactly when I visited Conrad – I had only read one thing of his, and that was a newspaper article. And if that had not been sent to me by a Press Cutting Agency, because of my name being mentioned in it, in which Conrad had said that a certain poem of mine would be read when radium would no longer be a wonder – if it had not been for this, I could have said that I had never read a line of Joseph Conrad.

That night, when it was getting late, I saw Conrad in such a way that I do not care to remember him under any other circumstances. We were all standing at the time, to wish Mrs. Conrad good night. And when Mrs. Conrad still continued her conversation with me, her husband stood there silently, holding his two hands, and with the most wonderful smile I had ever seen on a man's face. It was a smile full of kindly amusement and indulgence, as though he were the great father and we were his little children. He stood like this for a minute or two and then said – 'There, there, say good night, you are keeping the gentlemen standing.' Saying this, he bent his head, and, after kissing his wife's hand, he led her gently to the door. We will leave Conrad at that – standing with his face in the full light, the full light of his own spirit.

When I left Conrad he presented me with his last book, *Victory*. But although I thoroughly enjoyed it, I must confess that it was more from my low taste in Literature than my better taste; in the same way as I enjoy beer as well as wine, and am a good judge of either. For I found *Victory* to be sheer melodrama, and not a work of high art. And when I tried to repeat that wonderful dose of melodrama, by getting a copy of *Lord Jim*, I found that, although I struggled to the fortieth page, I could not get one page farther. So I am now waiting to read *Typhoon*, *Chance* and the *Nigger*, to find the hand of a master.

4: THE PHILOSOPHER

Who knows the perfect life on earth?
  It lies beyond this mortal breath;
It is to give the same kind thoughts
  To Life as we bequeath to Death.

It is to show a steadfast love;
  As faithful to our friends that live
As our dead friends are to ourselves –
  Sealed up from gossip, in the grave.

But who can lead this saintly life,
  When friends are false and men unkind;
And every man will cheat a man
  Whose trust, like faith in God, is blind.

Hang this pale fool, Philosophy!
  Kind hearts obey themselves, no other:
Why like a saint can I take pain
  And not inflict it on another?

★

I HAD now been living in London for several
months, and met quite a number of literary
men. But as some of them have left no striking
impression on my mind, and seeing that I am not
writing this book for the sake of mentioning

names – this being the case, I will remove them gently from my path, without giving them the cold shoulder.

On one occasion, when I had called on my publisher, my conscience was made to feel uneasy by his suggestion that I should call on the Shaws, to thank them personally for what they had done for me. Now, I had always wanted to do this, but had always been afraid of Shaw's gluttony for work. This fear was soon justified, for when I sent him a line proposing to call on him, he answered at once, inviting me to have tea with Mrs. Shaw and himself on the following day. But he finished up by saying that he was attending rehearsals, and would not have much time to spare. 'I am leading a dog's life,' he said – 'not that any dog would or could stand it.'

On the following afternoon I was at Adelphi Terrace and, seeing a small gate at the front of the stairs that led up into a flat, I rang the bell. It was not long before I was confronted by an Irishwoman who, before I could say a word, cried in a savage voice – 'He's not in!' Although I tried to explain that, in spite of not knowing either Mr. or Mrs. Shaw, yet, for all that, they had proved great friends to me, and I felt certain that they would be glad to see me. But the woman's face became harder and harder, and it did not even get softer when I said that I was expected there to tea. Strange to say, this bad beginning was followed by the most extraordinary welcome I have ever received anywhere; for the next minute a woman's head appeared over the banisters, and a simple, spontaneous voice cried - 'Is that you (calling me by name)? Come on, come on.' It was all so natural that I felt at home at once, and went up the stairs as though they were my own.

After this cordial greeting, it will not be surprising to hear that Mrs. Shaw and I were soon on the best of terms and talking without the least difficulty. This went on for some time, until Mrs. Shaw suddenly looked up into the air and said –'This is Mr. Davies.' Turning around at these words, I saw, to my astonishment, that a tall, bearded man was standing like a stone statue at my side, with a long arm extended in my direction. How he came there was a mystery, for I had not heard the least sound and, I may as well say here, my hearing is distinctly good. I had lived in lonely places where it was always wise to be on the alert for sounds, and to investigate – although it might only be a beetle crawling under the leaves.

But when I saw that man standing there, I had not the remotest idea of three people being present in that room. I began to think of trapdoors in the floor, which worked with wonderful ease, or the same kind of doors in the ceiling, to let people down on invisible wires. However, the grip of his hand proved that there was no illusion, and it was not long before he was saying how much we knew each other – through correspondence and mutual confidence – although we had never met until then.

Just before this meeting, I had been reading the poems of Clarence Mangan, and began to tell the Shaws of my great admiration for the 'Dark Rosaleen,' and some of that author's other pieces. 'Yes, yes,' said Shaw, when he heard this, 'but Tom Moore has written some good things too.' He then began to quote from Moore, and when his memory began to fail, Mrs. Shaw prompted him. And when Mrs. Shaw's memory failed, her husband came to the rescue. In this way they managed between them to recite quite a number of poems by Tom Moore.

I was rather surprised at this, to find that Shaw was one of the most poetical men I had ever met. I had always looked on him as a human philosopher and a master of Political Economy, and, on that account, had been in some fear of meeting him. And when at last he began to talk of his visit to a lonely lighthouse and its one lonely inhabitant, the silence of that perilous journey in a small boat, with only the sound of the waves beating its sides, and the rhymic splash of the men's oars as they rowed away from the wild coast – when I listened to this, I was more dumfounded than ever. 'Where,' thought I, 'is that cold practical thought, which is only common-sense, but which, coming at the psychological moment, when other people have lost their heads, reaches the height of a divine philosophy? Why is it that this one man in particular has the power at times to utter a little common-sense and make us see it for the first time?'

Shaw was there for about twenty minutes, and then had to rush off, having to attend a rehearsal of one of his own plays. But although he had come in a silent, mysterious way, as I have said, I was determined to keep a sharp eye on his departure. However, I am not quite certain how he left the room, for he appeared to glide and thin away, and I am not sure whether he opened the door at the end of the room, or passed clean through it like a ghost. With the exception of hearing his voice, I am positive that he made no other sound; either when he sat down or got up; either in his coming or his going, or in his use of the tea-things.

The Shaws had been very good to me as an unknown author. Not only had Shaw written a preface for my *Autobiography of a Super-tramp*, but Mrs. Shaw had also done everything she could in the matter of getting the book published. She paid for the type-setting and casting, and told me it was my own property. But when the Great War came, and I had no money to pay for the paper, printing and binding for a new edition, I had either to lose all my type and plates or let the book go out of print altogether. So I gave the machinery to my publisher, who then supplied the paper and covers for a new edition, paying me a royalty on each book

68

that was sold. However, the raising of my pension in that very year more than made amends for the loss of my plant.

Soon after the Shaws had done me this great kindness, I wrote to Mrs. Shaw, saying that I would like to dedicate a book of poems to them both. But Shaw did not like the idea of dedications, and here is his opinion, coming through his wife, who said that if her husband had been writing to me directly, he would have put it to me more nicely.

'Dedications be damned! Poetry is a very big thing, addressed to the whole world, and it should not be labelled with the names of individuals. It is like giving a soldier a cross for valour and then belittling it by putting the name of Queen Victoria on it. Besides, Davies doesn't understand about dedications. When my mother first came to London she innocently dedicated one of her songs to a certain officer who had sung it when it was only in MS. To her horror, he acknowledged the compliment by sending her a very nice letter enclosing a £10 note, and formally covering up the gift by asking her to give him credit for copies to that amount, in case he should need them. My mother, of course, sent back the money; and she took good care not to dedicate her songs to people again. Only yesterday there was an account in the papers of an Italian priest committing suicide because he dedicated a book to the Pope, and the Pope only sent him £4. The only dedications that are not liable to be misunderstood in this way are those dedications to a wife, or mother, or father, which have now become hackneyed. Davies mustn't dedicate his book to anybody. We should not misunderstand, but lots of other people would.'

As I have never had any idea or intention of writing a book of this kind, I have no notes in hand, and have to rely entirely on my memory. But I have been fortunate in finding the above remarks in a letter from Mrs. Shaw, which I had placed in a book she had sent me — *Selected Passages from the Works of Bernard Shaw*. With the exception of the Shaws, I have never in all my life written to anyone proposing a meeting, with the intention of writing about them afterwards; and that will account for a number of well-known names who are not mentioned in these pages.

Whatever people think of Shaw, judging by his work, it is certain, judging by the great number of young authors that have had their work read and criticized by him, that he is one of the most sympathetic men living. The only other heart I knew to match his is the heart of a woman — Alice Meynell. When I consider the number of writers who have told me of letters they have received from Bernard Shaw and Alice Meynell, I am amazed. Everywhere I go I meet them; some of them have had success, and others have failed. Only the other day a poet wrote to me from the country, sending me a little volume of poetry. And when I returned a few lines of encouragement, he wrote back to say that it was only once before that he had met with kindness — the other time was when Alice Meynell had written to him.

I did not meet Alice Meynell until a short time before her death, when a friend took me along with him on Armistice night. She had just finished a review of one of the older poets, and asked me if I did not think his work was sustained. As I did not have as good an opinion of that poet's work as I had of Alice Meynell's usually sound judgment, I answered – 'Yes, there is certainly something in his work that is sustained, but I don't know exactly what it is.' This caused her to give a slight laugh, but she did not press the matter more closely.

I may as well say here that I had never had the least wish to meet Alice Meynell, because of the great number of writers who had forced themselves on her, regardless of her own work and time; and the same thing applies to Thomas Hardy. It seems to me that the best respect we can show to a great writer is to keep out of his way and not waste his time, making it of no more value than our own. How often have I heard great beggars complain of their wasted time, when they have been detained in conversation by people who were more inquisitive than generous.

Still do I claim no man can reach
His highest soul's perfection,
Until his life, from day to day,
Deserves a dog's affection.

*

We will now go back to the Mont Blanc,
where Edward Garnett presided over the
midday meal. Now, after that meal, Edward
Thomas and myself would go along to the St.
George's Restaurant in St. Martin's Lane, where
there would be another gathering to tea, presided
over by Edward Thomas. The regular attendants
were Edward Thomas, Ralph Hodgson, myself,
and one or two others. Strange young writers came
occasionally, being invited by Edward Thomas after
he had reviewed their books in the various papers.

Hodgson was a man to my own mind, for we
both preferred to talk of dogs and prizefighters
instead of poets and poetry. He was very seldom
seen without his dog, and the same words could
be applied to him, with a little difference, as to
the Mary of our childhood days, when we read —

'And everywhere that Mary went,
The lamb was sure to go.'

73

The sight of Hodgson and his dog always reminded me of those words, altered to fit his particular case —

> 'And everywhere that Hodgson went,
>   The dog was sure to go.'

Not only did I like Hodgson for that — that I could exchange ideas with him on the noble art of self-defence — but that there was another strong bond between us, which was that he smoked the same common strong tobacco as I did. For that reason we could help each other out, in case one of us ran short. I may as well say here that I have now changed my tobacco, for I have discovered a tobacco that equals my old tobacco in strength and has the advantage of a fragrant odour. So that I can now puff big clouds into a lady's face, and cause her to smile instead of suffocate. But Hodgson, I believe, still sticks firmly and faithfully to the same old weed, saying that he would rather change his friends than change his tobacco.

But although Hodgson said, 'I would rather change my friends than my tobacco,' it must not be thought that his conscience was always satisfied with that. On one occasion, when we were both invited to meet some ladies at their club, Hodgson's conscience behaved so cowardly that he even betrayed one of his best friends. For when the ladies told us we could smoke, Hodgson, knowing the strong odour of his tobacco and mine, said, as we were filling our pipes – 'Don't mind Davies' tobacco, it is awfully strong.' This remark, of course, acted as a restraint on my smoking, and I had to puff too gently for my full enjoyment. Whereas Hodgson, who usually puffed enough smoke for two men, had his courage increased by my timidity, and made enough smoke for three. The only satisfaction I could take was to break up the party by leaving early, knowing that Hodgson must follow before the truth came out as to which smoker caused the most annoyance.

Only once, I believe, have Hodgson and I not agreed in our opinions. We had been talking of coloured men, and I, with the prejudice I had brought with me from America, was not speaking of them too kindly. On hearing this Hodgson said something about 'prejudice,' and giving them 'fair play.' When I heard this I was astonished, for even Hodgson had admitted that we in England were more lenient to coloured people than to our own. So I said, 'If I am prejudiced against them, you are prejudiced in their favour, and that is much worse. So when you say "fair play for coloured men," let me answer, "fair play for white men." '

However, this was a dangerous subject, and we changed it almost immediately.

At one time Hodgson used to come to my place to lunch once a week, bringing his bull-terrier along with him, for whom a special meal had been prepared. The dog knew this so well that he no sooner turned the corner of my street than it took all his master's strength to keep him in hand. And when they were in the house the dog used so much strength in entering the room that his master had to follow in the best shape he could command.

One day Hodgson was white with temper. It seems that a small black cat had chased the two of them up Charing Cross Road, and Hodgson had to run — not for his own life or his dog's — but for the cat's life. Hodgson knew that the cat was behind him, but the dog did not. So when he gave his dog more freedom to run, the dog took advantage and pulled harder and harder, until both master and dog were running for their lives. Seeing her enemies in full flight increased the cat's courage, of course, and she followed faster and faster, until she had chased them the whole length of Charing Cross Road. What made Hodgson so indignant was this – that Mooster, his big, strong bull-terrier, could have killed twenty cats in as many minutes, and yet he had to be made to run away from *one*, and a small one at that.

However, Hodgson soon got over this, and looking affectionately at his dog, said – 'Why doesn't Davies sell his books and buy a bull pup?'

This advice may sound amusing to others, expecially literary men, but to me it was quite a serious matter. For I would never think of keeping a dog or, for that matter, any other pet animal, unless I could give it close and proper attention; and it would only be as a married man that I would be able to do that. What has kept me from keeping pet animals has not been my indifference to them, but to my great love of them. My life has been in danger on several occasions, but I have always counted my adventure with a certain strange dog as one of my most trying experiences. This was in the wilds of America, when I had to threaten a dog for over ten minutes, to prevent him from becoming more friendly and making me his master. Under the circumstances, I persuaded myself that I acted wisely for the both of us, in giving that poor creature a chance to find a more prosperous master.

On one occasion we dined with one of Hodgson's best friends, who was also a great friend of mine. As Hodgson was a strict teetotaller, while we were drinking men, his friend and I began to wonder how Hodgson would be affected by drink. Seeing that Hodgson was such a furious and loud talker, and always gave one the impression that he was intoxicated, we came to the conclusion that drink would make him a melancholy whiner, and not the jolly, laughing man we saw at our side.

But we had no sooner brought this subject to an end than our friend, Hodgson's and mine, introduced the English novel in such a way that

I became a little alarmed. For he began to express himself like this – 'Now there lived down in Somersetshire a certain man, who was a Justice of the Peace and a Magistrate; that man's name was Henry Fielding, and he has been called "The Father of the English Novel." '

It was not long before he came to Richardson and others. When we were half-way through the dinner he was thoroughly enjoying himself on the subject of Dickens and Thackeray. At the end of the dinner he had come to Meredith and Thomas Hardy.

What Hodgson's real feelings were I cannot say, for he himself was a great and furious talker. That being the case, I feel certain that he could not have listened quietly and happily to the voice of another, for a whole hour too – not even when it was the voice of one of his very best friends. As for myself, being a man who always preferred to listen than to talk, and always happy if others saved me my tongue for drink and tobacco – as for myself, I was quite satisfied with what had happened. But when Hodgson and I were out of the restaurant and our mutual friend had gone, I said – 'Do you know, Hodgson, that we have

79

had a full and complete lecture on the English novel?'

When he heard this, Hodgson appeared to be rather uneasy, as though he had hoped that the fact had escaped my notice. However, true and faithful to his friends, Hodgson answered seriously indeed – 'Yes, Davies, and wasn't it jolly good too!'

Some time after this Hodgson and I went there again to dinner, again accompanied by a third friend – Mooster, his big, brown bull-terrier, who quickly won the admiration of the head waiter. For before either Hodgson or myself received one little morsel of food, that waiter had brought Mooster a large dish of bones, with the remark – 'This is yours, sir.' These bones the dog, with his strong, white dreadnoughts of teeth, crunched through with so much ease that we were all frightened at the sound. And it was no wonder that the gentleman who sat in the seat at the back of us was afraid to offer one word of complaint, when Mooster sat up and began to lick him all over his bald head. As the gentleman with the bald head did not appear to relish this as much as the dog, the latter had to be drawn back by force and quietly rebuked for his greed in wanting a second meal, when he had already had several pounds of meaty bones.

When we had finished dinner Hodgson asked me if I was in any hurry to get back home. On hearing that I was not, he proposed a walk, and off we went. But although I made every effort to start a conversation with Hodgson, and to sustain it, I failed every time. Sometimes, when I had asked him a question, and was expecting an answer, I saw, to my surprise, that Hodgson was five or six feet away from me, either in front or behind. At first I thought he must have had something serious on his mind and was unhappy. One moment we would be standing in the full light, and the next moment we would be standing in a dark doorway. One moment we would be in the main street, and the next moment in a dark, narrow alley. But although I could not account for this, I was determined not to question Hodgson, but to wait and find out the meaning for myself. However, I now began to realize that the dog was not following his master, but that the master was following his dog. I began to wonder why I was there at all. For instance, the dog

81   F

went where he liked and ignored the both of us; and his master could not give me the attention that was due to me as a friend and a companion, however much he would have liked to do so.

This strange behaviour of man and beast went on until we came to Carlton House Terrace, and it was now that I began to have some fear of the consequence. For it was soon obvious to me that we were trespassing on private property, and that Mooster was to blame for it. Not only that, but the houses, which had been in darkness until then, suddenly began to show lights in their porches and windows, and there were sounds of the opening and bolting of doors. Our presence had been discovered, that was certain; not because we made a great noise, but because the place had a churchyard quietness about it.

'Hodgson,' I said, 'we'll be arrested, for I believe we are trespassing.'

'It's all right now,' answered Hodgson in a happy voice, 'Mooster is very particular where he raises his leg, but it's all right now.'

It was now, for the first time, that I had the least idea of why we had undertaken that strange walk.

'Particular,' thought I, ' so I should think, seeing that we are in the neighbourhood of palaces and select clubs.'

The walk back home was much less exciting, for we all kept close together, Hodgson and I talking, and the dog listening to our conversation.

I HAVE two loves, and one is dark,
  The other fair as may be seen ;
My dark love is Old London Town,
  My fair love is the Country green.

My fair love has a sweeter breath,
  A clearer face by day; and nights
So wild with stars that dazzled I
  See multitudes of *other* lights.

My dark love has her domes, as round
  As mushrooms in my fair love's meadows;
While both my loves have houses old,
  Whose windows look cross-eyed at shadows.

*

I HAD now been living in London for some time
and, although I was still under the fascination
of certain sides of its life, such as its magnificent
shops, its fine old squares, its churches and other
public buildings, yet, for all that, I was beginning
to feel the need of a short change. The spring of
the year had come, and I could neither get pleasure from meeting friends nor from staying at
home and doing my best creative work. So one
fine Monday morning I started out for a two

weeks' walk, telling no one of my intention and leaving all my letters to accumulate until I returned.

My preparations for this journey were simple indeed, for I always had the free use of my two arms. In the first place I took a bath and put on an old clean shirt and a pair of clean socks. After that I took another light and clean shirt, which I rolled up as small as possible, and managed to get into my hip pocket. Then I took my razor, a comb, a piece of soap, a needle and thread, a toothbrush, a small nailbrush for my clothes and boots – all of which I wrapped in a handkerchief and which now filled a side pocket in my coat. In the other side pocket I carried my pipe, tobacco and matches.

Seeing me standing there, no one would think for one moment that I was equipped for a two weeks' journey. And, seeing that I would take another bath at the end of the first week and put on the clean shirt, discarding the old one for good – seeing that I would do this, I would, of course, have very little to encumber me during the second week. The same handkerchief would do for the whole time, for I would wash it as often as I liked in the wayside pools or streams, and dry it in a few minutes in the wind and sun as I walked along. My only extravagance on this journey would be to buy a new pair of socks at the end of the first week and throw away the dirty ones. Other things, contained in my other pockets, such as a lead pencil, a small book for scribbling in, a pocket-knife, money, etc., I need not mention, for these things were always with me. So when I started on my two weeks' journey I had the satisfaction of knowing that my looks did not betray me; and if I met a friend in the first hour or two, he would not know but what I was only out for a short walk.

The difference between a good walker and a bad one is that one walks with his heart and the other with his feet. As long as the heart is eager and willing, the strain on the body is not very important; and it is only at night, when his long journey is done, that a man's muscles feel swollen and stiff. This means that no man should go forth as a wanderer unless he is a true lover of Nature; for it is the ever-changing scenery that keeps his heart light until the end of his day's walk.

Nothing has given me more happiness in the

past than to spend the whole month of May in wandering about the country-side. I am not free for the first day or two of the care that my friends have called at my rooms in Town and found them unoccupied; and letters have been dropped into my letter-box that may require an immediate answer. But on the third day my new life brings me new thoughts, and I no longer think of friends, letters or enemies. Under a fine rainbow, whose arc encircles the whole world, there is no space for an enemy.

When I am in Town and meeting people almost every day, they seldom leave me without first trying to prejudice my mind against another. I could always say to myself, on their appearance – 'Here they come again, to take away a little more of my innocence.' How it would sweeten the lives of these dangerous gossips, and broaden their minds too, if they went out into the world alone for a month in every year.

It must not be thought from these words that when I go walking all my delight is in Nature, and that I am not curious to know something about the lives of other wanderers whom I meet on the road. For instance, I shall never forget the aggressive little bantam man I once met between St. Albans and Luton, who assured me that he had the power, by a few swift tricks, known only to himself, of bringing the biggest man flat to the earth in less than twenty seconds! And he had only just finished telling me this when we met a tall, fat gipsy, who inquired, in a civil voice, whether we had seen anything of his strayed pony.

'No,' answered my little bantam man, annoyed at the gipsy's height and the size of his belly – 'No, and if we had we would not give you any information.'

With these bitter words the bantam suddenly rushed forward, and with his two fists began to beat a wild tattoo on the gipsy's belly; and then, with the same lightning speed, sprang back to safety, expecting to see the giant fall flat to the earth. But to our surprise, instead of this happening, the gipsy only laughed, and put himself in the attitude to fight in earnest. I must confess that I was just as much surprised as my little bantam friend, for I had always thought that that place, especially when big, was the most vulnerable place to attack.

I was not quite quick enough to see whether the

bantam's fists sank into the man's belly as they would into a soft feather pillow, or whether the blows slid off like water from a duck's back — whichever it was, it was quite certain that the life within that round place was not disturbed in the least. In fact, the gipsy, to prove that he was nothing the worse for that vicious attack on his belly, stuck it farther out, as a challenge to my little bantam to repeat his performance.

This experience, and others that I have mentioned elsewhere, gives the Open Road a certain liveliness at times; while Nature still keeps her interest for a man when he travels alone.

But I have found that the majority of these tramps — who call themselves 'true travellers' — are not quite so pugnacious as the little chap I have just mentioned above. They talk loud and big, it is true, but they are really quite harmless when it comes to action. They are only ordinary mortals after all. That is to say — every man has the heart of a bull when he is meeting nothing but peaceful cows; but when the bull himself is met, we would all prefer to have no witness to our courage.

In spite of my knowledge of tramps, and my experience with them, I must admit that I was

once deceived by one of them in a most extraordinary way. The man's voice was so quiet, and
he expressed himself in so few words, that I could
not help thinking he must be a man of tremendous
power, and applied the proverb to him, that 'still
waters run deep.' Why are we so apt to do this,
seeing that proverbs are often foolish things to
listen to and almost always bear a second meaning? For instance, what does it matter whether
still waters run deep or shallow waters make much
noise — they are to be judged by their clearness and
absence from mud, and nothing else. We meet so
many quiet men that have nothing to say, and that
accounts for their silence. And we must admit that
a number of our loudest talkers are full of interesting ideas, although they use too many words to
express them.

But the thing that most impressed me with this
man, whom I have just mentioned, was not so
much his quiet voice and the few words he uttered,
but a peculiar way he had of opening one side of
his lips and showing a glint of white teeth. This
made him look a very dangerous man indeed.
And matters were not helped much when the first
words he said were — 'My parents were both born

in England, but I have enough foreign blood in my veins to make myself dangerous if anyone tries to take a liberty with me.'

I was so impressed by this man's looks and manner, that I really expected to see him, in case of emergency, turn into a human porcupine, with his body suddenly bristling with scores of knives, daggers and stilettos. The glint of this man's white teeth could mean nothing else, I felt certain of that. 'If we are attacked by anyone, even a dozen men,' thought I, 'no one will be able to touch or lay hands on this man; and my own safety, standing behind his back, will be absolutely certain, and be a matter of more amusement than fear.'

All this was foolish for, that very night, when there was a skirmish in the lodging-house kitchen, in which every person was forced to take a part, because of so many people being in a limited space – what happened then? This new friend of mine, instead of bristling like a porcupine, vanished as mysteriously as a white butterfly – a butterfly that has not been seen to leave the open light. The very fact that he had been able to do so, shows how much fear had quickened his wits;

ιor if he had not left the room while the quarrel was young and before a blow had been struck, it is certain that he would not have been able to do so in the confusion that followed. Yes, he not only vanished, but did not even have enough courage to return after the battle was over and claim his bed, which he had already paid for.

What I like so much about meeting these strange people on the Open Road, is their plain and simple characters, which can be known, as a rule, in a few short hours. Things are different in our higher grades of society. When I am asked if I know a certain man, and answer 'Yes,' I often feel inclined to add with a touch of irony — 'but only his face.' For I certainly cannot understand why one writer, who professes a great admiration for women, has never written a love-song, and never uttered a fine phrase of a woman's grace or beauty. While another author, who is fond of drink, has never written a drinking song, or said one word in praise of drink or against it. They make litera-ture a mask to hide their real personality, and how can they expect to attain that strength which only comes through honesty and sincerity?

But the simple people we meet on the Open Road

93

never go to theatres, and their real life never reflects the artificial life of the stage. They always seem to behave naturally, and never appear to be self-conscious and affected. They never affect the manners of their betters — unless they imitate them among themselves for their own amusement.

SHALL I have jealous thoughts to nurse,
When I behold a rich man's house?
Not though his windows, thick as stars,
    Number the days in every year;
I, with one window for each month,
    Am rich in four or five to spare.

But when I count his shrubberies,
His fountains there, and clumps of trees,
Over the palings of his park
    I leap with my primeval blood;
Down wild ravines to Ocean's rocks,
    Clean through the heart of No-man's Wood.

*

IT will be remembered that I was ready to start
on a two weeks' journey, and the month was
May. My intention was to take a train to Bristol,
and then to walk back to London, coming through
Bath, Marlborough and Newbury, and other
towns on the way. As I had no intention of
writing my experiences, and have taken other
journeys since then, I cannot remember much
of that one in particular. The journey was
taken for health and pleasure, and the only excitement I needed was to stand alone on a

small bridge and look down into the water, or to listen to the skylarks and walk in their shower of melody.

However it was quite obvious that I was not a professional tramp, and it was impossible to pass the numerous beggars that came along without being begged for either money or tobacco. But although I hardly ever refused one of them, I soon began to see that the Bath Road had far too many of them for my liking. So I came to the conclusion that it would be much cheaper to find a tramp who was going my way, and to have his protection against his fellows. For of course no tramp would stop and speak to me when he saw that I was already in possession of another. It was certainly cheaper to do this, although I gave my fellow-traveller a few pennies when I parted from him.

In this way I picked up with a companion at one time, just after I had left Bath, of one of the most interesting beggars I have ever met; and I soon had to make up my mind that he was the first and only one of his kind, and a genius among his fellow-travellers. To all appearances he was a beggar, and yet he carried something in his hand that distinguished him from every other beggar I had ever seen— it was an umbrella. If he had had others, I, of course, would have understood that he was an umbrella-mender, or, to use the words of the Open Road — 'a mush-fakir.' But this was not the case, for all he seemed to possess was this one umbrella, and a brand-new one at that. However, I came to the conclusion that he had either found it or stolen it, and would get rid of it for a few pence at the earliest opportunity. Under the circumstances, I decided that my association with a possible thief might lead to an unpleasant break in my journey. But when the man spoke to me and walked at my side, I thought no more of that, and began to question him about his strange career.

In a few minutes he had told me all. He was a money-beggar, it seems, and not a food-beggar, and he seldom called at private houses. 'If I succeed in selling an umbrella to a farmer, an innkeeper, or one of his customers I get at least a shilling for it and sometimes two,' he said. 'And if they cannot spare that amount, they give me a penny or two because they are amused and admire the trick.'

'But don't you have to buy the umbrellas?' I asked innocently.

On hearing this my companion gave a short laugh and, placing the umbrella in my hand, said — 'Have a look.'

It was then, for the first time, that I saw the umbrella was a dummy and all wood. It was made from the straight branch of a small tree cut just above the knot and shaped by a sharp knife until it was like an umbrella. It had then been smoothed by pieces of glass and sandpaper. After this certain parts were left in their natural colour, and other parts had been painted black, the result being that it looked exactly like a closed umbrella.

I came to the conclusion that this strange traveller could sell his umbrellas as fast as he could make them, and his only expense was an occasional tin of black paint and a penny sheet of sandpaper. Many an innkeeper would buy one of them for the sake of future amusement, when he would offer an umbrella to a customer who was going home on a wet day. And many a happy customer of the monied class would like to take one of them home to his wife or daughters. And yet the making of one of these umbrellas was so simple that anyone being once shown, could make one with ease in about an hour.

I don't know whether this man looked on me as a prospective buyer or not, but I certainly intended to give him something before I left him. However, this was not to be, for soon after this we came across three young sportsmen, who were laughing and talking outside an inn. As soon as we reached them, my companion, without telling me anything of his intention, left my side immediately and joined their company, while I walked on. When I looked back, after I had gone some distance, he was still there, and one of the youngsters had the umbrella in his hand, deeply interested it seemed. And when I looked back again, after walking another forty of fifty yards, I saw the same young sportsman leading the way into the inn, while the others followed, including my late companion. That was the last I saw of him. As I went my way I had not the least doubt but what the umbrella would be sold for a couple of shillings, and that my late companion would also receive a bellyful of ale.

But life is continually changing, and if I passed

99

that way now, in the year 1924, it is hardly likely
that I would meet another man like that, carrying
a dummy umbrella. The workhouse tramp is still
left, but the ingenious beggar is passing away, in
the same way as the cries of London and the carol
singers at Christmas, and other old customs.
Look at that grand old Welsh custom, when
young couples were allowed and encouraged to
court in bed between the blankets – who hears of
it now? This pleasant custom might have continued to the present day had it not been for
certain men who were prophets – but not bards –
sending up a loud cry that the land was already full
of bastards. But it seems that such a fine custom
should have been discontinued because of a few
accidents of that kind, and that war should be
allowed to continue, in which such accidents are
too common to mention. What was a shame in
times of Peace seems to have been noble in times
of War.

Yes, life is continually on the change, and it is
almost impossible, in these days, for any man to
keep his own individuality. If he writes love songs
about cuddling a pretty girl, he is told seriously
to avoid those pretty toys and study the deeper

problems of life; and yet the cuddling of a pretty girl has often led to a serious problem indeed. If he writes too much about humanity, his work is called sordid and dull; and if he writes too much about Nature, it is called lifeless and pretty. Not only that, but so much of this criticism is false and not to the point. For instance, if I sent the following poem to the press, it would be returned, and I will tell you why — although I must say that most of my things are accepted by either one editor or another:

Come away, Death, make no mistake,
   There's no one in that house to die;
She's young and strong, though suffering pain,
   And waits to hear her first-born's cry.

'Nay,' answered Death, 'there's no mistake,
   I've been to this same house before;
Though no one saw a corpse come out,
   Or any mourner at the door.

'I've been to this same house before,
   I know it well from any other:
And now I come again, to see
   A dead-born child destroy its mother.'

Now if I sent this poem to an editor it would probably be returned, and another, whose subject was a butterfly or bird, a daisy or a tree, would be accepted. The reason for this is that I have been labelled as a Nature poet, whom the deeper problems of life does not concern. For that reason I am not allowed to give my critics the lie, but must stick to my butterflies, my bees and my birds. The above subject is one for Thomas Hardy, with his interest in the deeper things, and not for a Nature poet – but why? Every poet is a man of moods, otherwise he would be dull indeed.

But let us return to the great Open Road, which some people will find more interesting than these remarks on poets and poetry. I had now been walking for several days and, forgetting all about literature and the business side of life, I was thoroughly enjoying my freedom. I would have liked to have spent the whole summer in that way, going from place to place, and putting up at the various inns. It must be remembered that the month was May, and if a bird could not sing it danced, because of the great light that was in the air.

On one occasion, when I was entering a small

town, towards evening, I was spoken to by a rather rough and dirty looking beggar, who, after saying that he would have to pay 'sixteen farthings for a feather,' informed me that he was a 'stever' short.

From this I gathered that his bed would cost him fourpence and, only having threepence towards it, he was a penny short. He did not appear to be a very interesting type of beggar and judging by his ragged clothes and the amount of hair on his head and face, did not seem to be very successful in his profession. However, it did not take me long to oblige him in that small matter and, after a few words, we parted. His first question was whether I belonged to the town I was going to.

'No,' I answered, 'but if I can get accommodation at one of the hotels, I intend to stay there for the night.'

After hearing this he left, thanking me for my kindness and hoping we would meet again in the morning – a hope that was not mine.

Not long after this I was booked for the night in the best hotel in the place, not being able to get accommodation elsewhere. This was an expensive part of my journey, and not to my liking. However, market day had brought its visitors, and the little town only had a limited amount of sleeping accommodation for strangers. So I preferred to accept the conditions, instead of paying a few pence to go by train to the next town, which was too far away for an additional walk.

When I entered this fine hotel to inquire if I could be put up for the night, I thought it would be wise to make a straightforward little speech at once, with the object of preventing the landlord from deciding against me. For as I was not driving up to his door in a coach or car, or was mounted on a horse, and had no more visible property than the clothes I wore and the walking-stick I carried in my right hand – this being the case I thought it would be advisable to let him know the reason, and to account for having no bag or luggage. So I told him at once that I was taking a walking-tour through the country, for a few days only, and being lame in one leg, had to travel as light as possible.

I don't know what impressed this landlord, whether it was my simple words or a good tweed cloth, but he was certainly very civil. Perhaps he was quite indifferent to these things, and was only pleased at the thought of letting one of his best rooms. Sometimes I thought he was under the impression that I was a rich London merchant or one of the nobility, and was respecting me accordingly. And when I had called for a drink and invited him to join me — at my expense, of course — he became more pleasant than ever. When I came to consider the matter more closely, I came to the conclusion that what impressed this landlord most was this — that I had not asked him one question about his charges, as though I was ready to pay him any amount he liked to ask, in or out of reason. The landlady also appeared to be very gracious, being, I suppose, impressed by the effect I had made on her husband.

When I went to bed that night, the landlord himself lighted me up the stairs to my room, and when he left he said in a very pleasant voice — 'This is your room, sir. I hope you will sleep comfortable and well. I wish you good night, sir.'

'What pleasant people,' thought I; 'how pleasant it is to hear such kind voices.'

The next morning I was down to breakfast just after nine o'clock, but what a change had come over my good host and his wife! For after wishing me 'good morning,' coldly, they both looked at each other in a strange way. It was apparent that they had something on their minds, and neither one of them had the courage to speak out openly. The man looked flushed and confused, but his wife's face was hard and set. 'What is the matter?' thought I. I remembered everything that had happened on the previous night, up to the very last minute, and nothing seemed to have gone wrong. However, I was soon to have an explanation, or at least the beginning of one.

'A man who calls himself your friend,' said the landlord's wife, at last, 'has just called to see if you are still here or gone away. And when I told him that you had not yet left your room, he said he would call again in about half an hour's time.'

'There must be some mistake,' I answered, 'for I have no friends in this place, and am travelling alone. What kind of man was he?'

'One of the dirtiest and most ragged men I have ever seen,' answered the landlady.

When I heard this I at once understood everything, and I felt very sorry indeed for bringing, without the least intention, so unwelcome a visitor to their house, which they conducted so respectably.

The next moment I explained everything to the landlord, telling him exactly what had happened. 'But how did he know I was staying at this hotel?' I asked.

'No doubt he made inquiries at other places,' answered the landlord, 'and was determined to find you.'

But although I did not leave my hotel until nearly eleven o'clock, the tramp had not returned, and I never saw him again.

I don't know what the landlord's first thoughts had been when this dirty-looking tramp gave a description of me and, hearing that I was there, referred to me as his friend. Very likely he thought that we were two swindlers who were playing some shady game in the various country towns; and, although one was well dressed and the other was ragged, we were both equals in each other's eyes.

When I paid my bill, which was quite reasonable, the landlord had returned to his respectful manner, and his wife, too, appeared to be sorry for what had happened. For I had, of course, expressed the deepest regret that I had been the cause of so unwelcome a visitor. In the end they blamed me gently for being too kind and generous to undeserving tramps; 'which,' said they, 'comes of your innocence of that kind of life.'

When I left the hotel I was soon asking myself this question — 'What was it that impressed this landlord so much that he thought I must be a superior person, and yet so little impressed a ragged tramp that he had called himself my companion and friend?' But there was no accounting for this, seeing that we all have different ideas as to who is a gentleman and who is not. We are still no wiser than the little boy who answered his teacher that 'a gentleman is a man who wears a gold watch and chain'; and then, seeing the look of disappointment on his teacher's face, added quickly — 'and loves Jesus.'

I was now more than half-way between Bristol and London, and had already passed through Savernake Forest. For some reason or other, I found the forest lifeless and monotonous, in the same way as I have found Epping Forest. I could not imagine that the Savernake Forest contained a mystery ; and that being the case, it was less interesting to me than many a small wood or thicket I had seen on the hill-side or in the hollows of fields.

There was nothing very exciting after this; and although I was impressed by the steady increase of human life and the additional noise and bustle as I advanced nearer and nearer to London, yet for all that I cannot say that the change was unpleasant. There was no doubt but what this journey through the quiet country had so increased my health and steadied my nerves that I was now better able to endure the noise and clamour of a city, even as big as London.

So I entered London, thinking of another soon, but not deciding where I would go, or how long I would take to make it.

ONE night, when I was sleeping all alone,
Close to a forest, far from any town,
Up with a cry I started – what was that
Which shook me here, as though I were a rat!
I met a black man in the morning light,
Who said – and fear had made him ashen white –
'Where were you when this earth of ours
Shook terribly in the early hours?'
And shall the Himalayas and the Alps
Wriggle like worms, when the Earth gulps
Half the Pacific in one breath!
Think if the death
Of countless people –
When the bells in each surviving steeple
Toll for the dead in every shaken land,
Without a touch from any mortal hand;
Until this Earth lies down again to rest,
And sleeps without a conscience in her breast.
Is not the fear of this sufficient then
That War must cease and Friendship come to men?

★

WAR is a cruel thing: it is as cruel as the
lightning, when it strikes at eyes it has
already blinded once. When the Great War had
been going on for years, and there were still no

signs of a peaceful settlement, there was not a free man left in the whole country. The rationing of certain commodities made it difficult to change our surroundings, and the incivility and brutality of shopkeepers made life unpleasant indeed. For while our soldiers were fighting abroad, with shot and shell, the people at home were conducting a civil war among themselves, insulting each other on every occasion they met. Friends quarrelled without reason, and all because of the high strain on their nerves. If I discussed the war with a friend, I never knew how he would take it; and to say that the best citizens in America were Germans, as I firmly believed, was dangerous indeed — though I never feared to say so.

It is only now, when the War has been over for years, that I realize how terrible were those days; when thousands went mad, and almost every one reached the point of madness and were just saved in time by the declaration of Peace. Even for a year after the Great War was over I feared that my own mind was injured enough to have lost all its power; like a bird that is injured in the wing and lives to hop and chirp, but no longer can fly and come into full song. I had fears that this would be the case with myself, as soon as I began to set my brain to make substance for a dream, or command it to give a plain and solid fact the appearance of a strange invention. Yes, many and many a time had I crossed the street to avoid speaking to some one I knew; and then, because he passed on without looking my way, cursed him for giving me a cold snub. But I was much nearer to madness than this, as will be seen.

At the beginning of the Great War I was friendly with an intelligent German girl, who was soon to be deported with others of her nationality. She may have been a dangerous spy, but she never gave me cause to think so. She defended her own country, naturally, in the same way as I defended mine.

'This fight between England and Germany,' I said, 'is a contest between a fighter and a boxer. The boxer scores points at the beginning, as Germany is doing now; but the fighter takes punishment and reserves his strength for a great onslaught, and wins in the end.'

My German girl friend listened to this quite calmly, and then said – 'But if a nation can fight as well as box, which is the case with Germany, will it not triumph over the nation that can fight and not box?'

This was our first battle of words, and, as I had the worst of it, I made another attempt. I compared the fight between England and Germany as a fight between a bull-dog and a collie; which begins in favour of the quicker collie, and ends in the terrible triumph of the bull-dog dragging the collie's dead body over the stones. 'This bull-dog tenacity of England must win in the end,' I said.

But the German girl did not appear in any way alarmed at these words, and answered calmly – 'Yes, but unfortunately for us all Germany has the same bull-dog tenacity.'

How often have I thought of these words, seeing that the War lasted so many years, and might have gone on much longer had not Germany been threatened by the millions of America.

As I have already said, we were nearly all on the verge of madness before the end of the War. In my own case this madness took an extraordinary turn, for I persuaded myself that I was being annoyed and persecuted by my neighbour. This affected me so seriously at last that I thought every little sound, the moving of furniture or the poking of a fire, was meant to annoy me. My ears were open to the very slightest sounds, and I blamed my neighbour for them all, in spite of my knowledge that the old walls had been hollowed by mice which went to and fro at all hours of the day and night.

When I heard a very small sound, I said to myself – 'How artful and malicious she is! That little sound is only to let me know that she is still there, and to get ready for a greater nuisance to follow.' And when she played the piano after that, I felt certain that she had only made that first little noise as a mistress in the art of cruelty, to warn me of the more terrible noises that would follow.

Now when I thought I had been cruelly annoyed and persecuted for over three months, I made up my mind to see into the matter, and went to see a lawyer about it. But after a month of correspondence and interviews, nothing seemed to have been done to abate the nuisance, and I soon had to pay a bill for several pounds.

After this failure I tried the police, and was visited off and on by a number of plain-clothes detectives; to each of whom I gave a glass of wine or whisky, and received in exchange a hearty handshake and a knowing wink. But after this my next-door neighbour got worse, ten times worse than she had ever been. So I took advantage of my name as an author and procured an introduction to the Chief of Police at Scotland Yard; and to him I accused the other police of bribery, saying that they had informed my neighbour of my complaints and made her worse. For I felt certain in my mind that these detectives had interviewed her, and that she had given them money — which I had not — so as to be allowed to continue her annoyance.

I found the Chief of Police to be kind and full of sympathy, and he promised to do all he could to help me, although he could not see exactly what could be done. 'The house is a brothel,' he said, 'and we have already raided it once and deported two of its inmates. But now, it being war time, we cannot very well deport these people to Belgium, where they belong, because that country is now our ally. So, since these people must be allowed to remain here for the time being, they will still be the same nuisance wherever they are. But I promise to do what I can to help you.'

Now that very night, after I had seen the Chief of Police at Scotland Yard, I was visited by a certain detective, who had been to see me on several occasions before. But this man had no sooner seated himself in my room than he began, to my astonishment, to tell me of his own troubles. For instead of inquiring about my next-door neighbour, whether she was behaving better or worse, he began to tell me of his own loss of sleep in the early morning, after he had been working all night. It seems that an Italian organ-grinder lived next door to him, and played his organ for a quarter of an hour or more early every morning, to see if it was in good condition for the day's work. 'And there is no law to stop that man from doing so,' said the detective.

When I heard this, I asked myself, of course – 'If this man, who represents the Law, has no power to help himself, how can I expect him to help me!'

But although this news surprised me, the news that followed almost took away my breath. 'We have had orders,' continued my kind friend, the detective, 'to keep an eye on number 14.'

'No, no,' I said, hastily, 'you mean number 15,

and not 14. My next-door neighbour is number 15, but *I* am number 14.'

'There is not the least mistake,' he answered, 'our orders are to keep a sharp eye on number 14.'

'But this is all foolish,' I said, 'for when the shop closes at night, I am the only one that is left on the premises.'

However, in spite of all I could say, the man still maintained that his orders were to keep a sharp eye on number 14.

This was all a mystery to me at the time; but when I consider the matter now, in after years, I have come to the conclusion that the police were either afraid that my neighbours would murder me, or that I would murder them, and thought it easier and wiser to watch me instead of them.

When I heard the detective say this, that *my* house was to be watched and not my neighbour's, I was so surprised and annoyed that I could not help telling him that there was a saying that 'the Law was an ass,' and that I was now convinced that that was so.

'You say that you can't stop a nuisance?' I asked, as he was leaving.

'That's just what I do say,' he answered.

'Well,' I continued, 'if you have no power to prevent my neighbour from being a nuisance, you will have none to prevent me, if I become a greater nuisance – will you?'

'What are you going to do?' he asked, rather anxiously.

'Come and see me in a week's time,' I answered, 'and you will find that my neighbour is much more quiet, and it will all be my own doing.'

Now the nuisance I complained of took many forms, but the principal one was that my neighbour, who slept through the early part of the day, sat up all night until about four o'clock in the morning, and played the 'Marseillaise' on a piano. 'This being the case,' thought I, 'why should I not sit up after four o'clock in the morning, when she is tired, and keep her awake with a far more rousing and formidable tune, namely, 'The March of the Men of Harlech'?

In less than an hour after having this idea, I was back in the house with a common cheap gramophone, with one record only – 'The Men of Harlech.'

That night my neighbour was as noisy as ever, for she played the 'Marseillaise' and other things from nine o'clock in the evening until half-past three the following morning. But although I lay awake all that time, I was still a happy man, for I knew what was to follow. After half-past three it was all quiet, but I waited until four o'clock, to give my neighbour a chance to settle down. When the clock struck four, I got out of bed and the first thing I did was to throw a heavy flat-iron into the empty grate, so that the sudden noise would wake her first, to prepare her for 'The Men of Harlech.' 'The Men of Harlech' was played once, but there was no response from my neighbour in the next house. It was played the second time and then I heard movements, for the wall that divided us was thin. But after I had played my national anthem for the third time, there came a hard banging on the wall, followed by a torrent of abuse. Her English words were so bad, and so little to be mistaken, that it almost frightened me to think of what she must have called me in her native tongue, which I did not understand. But in spite of this, I played ' The Men of Harlech' once more, before I got back into bed, happy with my first result.

The effect of this was seen on the following

night, for although she played the 'Marseillaise' up to twelve o'clock, and then gave the wall a terrific thud of defiance – it ended with that. And as I was now satisfied that her malicious spirit was broken, I let 'The Men of Harlech' rest. But I don't know what happened on the third night, whether she was drunk or was determined not to surrender – all I know is that she became as noisy as ever. So I waited again until four o'clock, and once more I attacked the 'Marseillaise' with 'The Men of Harlech,' which I now played six times in succession. That was the end of our little war. For although she strongly resented this by throwing things against the wall and abusing me with her tongue, yet for all that the house soon became so quiet that I did not know whether it was inhabited or not.

I have often wondered whether the poor woman was suffering from nerves, and meant no personal harm at all. But as my own nerves were also in a terrible state, I could not be expected to be as kindly and generous as I would be now. For instance, although the police had told me that the woman belonged to a certain class, yet, being an unmarried man, I was more prejudiced in her favour than against her, and would make a poor and indifferent inspector of morals. I had already told the police this, and only wanted them either to persuade or force her to conduct her house more quietly and not annoy her neighbours.

The great difficulty in a matter of this kind is that we have no means of knowing the truth, whether people are only naturally noisy or whether they are noisy from spite. If it is the former the kindest and wisest thing to do is to let them have their own way by going to live elsewhere. But when we think people are against us, and are annoying us from spite, the spirit is in us to fight back and show our right to live where we like.

I have often thought of the delightful little comedy that could be made out of an episode of this kind. Any young dramatist is welcome to it if he is capable of working it out. For although my opera is still unacted, and I am not allowed to add the name of dramatist to my name of poet, yet for all that I have already had some of my ideas *stolen* for the Stage.

The little bit of comedy I have mentioned would only consist of one scene, in which two bedrooms are seen one above the other. The man who sleeps in the room below will be nervous, suspicious, and with a strong sense of being persecuted. The man in the room above will be good-natured and innocent, but naturally clumsy and noisy. The scene opens with the man below, who has just gone to bed. While he is undressing he does nothing but abuse other people, saying that he cannot get a wink of sleep owing to the noise made by his neighbour, which is all done out of malice and petty spite.

Not long after this the top-floor man comes home, and mounts the stairs to his room. He is a big, heavy, good-natured fellow, and, being out of breath when he reaches his room, falls heavily into a chair. When the man in the room below hears this, he begins at once to curse and swear. This swearing does not escape the other, for he begins to say — 'I wonder what is the matter with that poor fellow downstairs; he always appears to be muttering to himself.'

Saying this he begins to knock the dust out of his pipe, using the grate for that purpose. On hearing this the man downstairs shouts out, 'Why don't you hammer and thud, instead of making those cowardly, tantalizing little noises to annoy me!'

'He has them properly to-night,' says the man above, hearing his neighbour's voice, but not hearing the words.

After a while the man upstairs begins to take off his boots and, as soon as he has one in hand, drops it on the floor.

This causes another outburst of temper from his neighbour below, which is so violent that the man above begins to get frightened, saying – 'The poor fellow is going mad.'

With these words he begins to puff at his pipe in no great hurry to take off his other boot.

But while he is smoking quietly and thinking with all kindly feeling of his strange neighbour, that man is seen sitting up in bed with his ears open and his eyes staring with terror, for he knows that the man upstairs has another boot to drop, and has only dropped one. At last he can bear the terrible suspense no longer and, looking up into the ceiling, shrieks – 'Ho, there, you flaming swine! When are you going to drop that other boot!'

These things may sound amusing now, but during the War it was quite common to meet people who had the red light of danger before their eyes all the time, and whose ears were affected by the least sound. I remember one evening during that time when the star Venus shone particularly bright, and how a number of people could not be persuaded that it was a star. Thinking it was another engine of war, they went whispering to each other — 'What light is that!' They connected everything they saw with the Great War, and every thunderstorm was another bombardment by the enemy.

On one occasion, when I was walking in Hyde Park, a lady caught me by the arm and, pointing to the sky, where a thin moon was showing part of its rim behind a cloud, exclaimed — 'Look, there's an airship; does it belong to Germany or England?'

But although I assured her that it was only the moon, she shook her head and hurried away to find a place of safety, I suppose.

When I walked the streets of London, after the War had been going on for years, and saw how the lonely women in black increased in numbers, being the widows and mothers of soldiers, I could not help judging life by them; and looking on every soldier as a dead lover, with a happy and unsuspecting girl at his side.

ALL from his cradle to his grave,
Poor devil, man's a frightened fool;
His Mother talks of imps and ghosts,
His Master threatens him at school.
When half a man and half a boy,
The Law complains of his high blood;
And then the Parson threatens him
With hell, unless baptized for good.
Soon after, when a married man,
He fears the humours of his Spouse;
And, when a father, fears to spend
One shilling that his Babes might lose.
Then comes Old Age, Lumbago, Gout,
Rheumatic Pains that ache and sting:
All from his cradle to his grave,
Poor devil, man's a frightened thing.

*

A MAN has enough trouble in his life, in a
natural way, without having the best years
of it spent in a war. And, strange to say, although
a Christian belief is more necessary at that time
than any other, yet that is the very time when it
fails; and people become bitter and cold in their
complaint of the God they once worshipped, and
now calls merciless. It is most difficult to expect

a woman to put her trust in God when she is left alone in the world, having lost her husband and three or four sons.

I am not what might be called a Christian man, and yet I would not be called an Atheist. I do not like the company of unbelievers; not because I disagree with their opinions, but because they are loud and vulgar, and their opinions are shouted to all comers, whether we are interested or not. Not only that, but if people are happy in a certain belief, why attack it? Surely there is no more virtue in trying to take the joy out of a man's soul than there is in taking the bread out of his mouth. However, although I am not a Christian man, I still have my own ideas of a future state. It is this — that if we are hunted and pursued in this life by malicious enemies, so, in the life to come, it is we that will be the hunters and our enemies the hunted. This idea comes from no vindictive spirit, for I certainly have no desire or hope that such will be the case. It comes from the knowledge that I have never wilfully done harm to anyone on earth, either man, woman or child. My capacity for taking punishment has been tremendous, but the spirit to inflict it on another was not given to me at birth. But in this new life to come, it will be the decree of the reigning powers that I shall ride on the backs of my enemies, and they will live in fear of me from hour to hour. This will go on until we die again and enter into another new state of life. For there is probably more states of life than one or two; and even in our next life to this, we will not be much wiser than we are now, to know what extraordinary life will be the end of all.

When this terrible world war was about half-way through, it can be said with certainty that there was scarcely one idle life in all England. The way in which our rich and fashionable women devoted their lives to the war was extraordinary in its unselfishness, and there were no idle rich, regardless of either age or sex. In saying this I do not forget the old 'Farmhouse' in Southwark, the common lodging-house in which I lived when I published my first book. At the beginning of the War it was supposed, like other houses of its kind, to consist of social outcasts, about ninety men in all; wasting their lives by standing in the gutters and selling papers and other trifles, or doing odd jobs at the different markets. The roll

I

of honour for that house of ninety social outcasts was twenty men!

One scheme to get funds towards the War, which was started by these ladies in high life, was particularly successful. It was to get together a number of poets to read their own work in some large drawing-room, which would be lent for the occasion. Tickets would be sold at a high price, so that at the end of the performance there would be a clear sum of several hundreds of pounds. For, of course, there would be no expense, unless it were a few pounds for printing programmes. But even these little sheets were sold for twenty and thirty times their worth, and it was all a part of the scheme to realize a larger sum.

The first meeting of this kind was held at Byron's old house in Piccadilly, with Augustine Birrell in the chair; and among the readers were Yeats and Belloc, who read their own poems; while two or three well-known actors recited the works of others.

Now it must be remembered that I am a very shy man, but not having courage to refuse help in a good cause, I allowed my name to be entered for that event. I had not the remotest idea of what would happen, for up till then I had never once read my own work aloud to anyone. However, I had the consolation to think that although people might think that I was a very bad reader they would not be able to say that I was a very bad poet.

At last the terrible day came, and it was not long before I was a part of that packed audience, waiting for my name to be called as the next reader. The meeting had opened with a witty speech by the chairman, after which Yeats read some of his most beautiful poems, which made the beginning a great success. Others followed, and then came two or three bad readers – who were not bad poets – and the audience began to show less enthusiasm. And when my name was called at this critical time, I was almost in a state of collapse, because of the failure of the men who had just read and the coldness of the audience. For, seeing that I had never before been on a public platform, and had never once taken a lesson in elocution, how could I feel otherwise?

However, it was not long before I was on the platform and, setting my eyes on my manuscript, was determined not to raise them again until my reading was over. But I had no sooner finished reading my first poem than the audience began to cheer, a thing they had not done before; and the chairman, who had been sitting silently in his chair, during the other readings, began to show his approval by saying every now and then — 'Yes, yes; ah, yes,' with almost as much excitement as the audience. One of the poems caused such a stir that I did not know what to do. A small group of young men began to cry out my name, and two or three ladies raised their voices to a higher pitch, crying — 'The Moon! The Moon!' which was the name of the poem I had just read. I need hardly say that when I had finished there were loud cries of 'Encore,' and I was sent back to read again, just as I was escaping through an open door.

When I was standing at the back of the audience, after I had done reading, and ready to slip away, a tall lady came up to me, and, saying that she was Clara Butt, congratulated me on my successful reading, and asked me if I would give her my MS. poems. But I told her that two of the poems were new, and I had no other copies of them, which disappointed her, I believe. However, I sent her a book of poems in a few days after, but have had no cause to think she ever read them.

I have said that when I stood on the platform I set my eyes on my MS., without the courage to raise them. But during the clamour, when the enthusiasm was greatest, I looked up once, for about one second, and it was during that very short time that I saw a most remarkable sight. For at the very back of the audience, I saw a round, smiling light, and it was a woman's face. It could not be seen by anyone else, only the two men that faced the audience, the chairman and myself. That the beauty of one woman should show like that, when the room held other women who were famous for their beauty, is hardly to be conceived. If I had been a lover and was looking for the face I loved most and found it, people would smile at my exaggeration and understand it. But as I am not certain, even to the present day, who the face belonged to, it will be understood that I am not exaggerating its beauty. It stood out by itself, a clear, distinct light, and made its surroundings uninteresting and dark. When I mentioned this to a friend of mine, some time after the event, he said it was the face of a certain

133

well-known actress who is famous for her beauty.

Not long after this there was another reading, at which Yeats read again, followed by others. But just before Yeats began to read, a certain poet whose turn had not come, got up and walked into an ante-room. I would not have taken much notice of this had it not been for an American 'poet, who said — 'Do you notice that?'

'Yes,' I answered, 'I suppose it is too warm in this room, and he has gone to that window for a little fresh air.'

'No, no,' said the American poet, 'it is not that; it is because Yeats and he are not very friendly.'

'Why?' I asked.

'I don't know exactly,' answered the American poet, 'but I believe it is through sitting together on so many committees.'

This made me register another important fact in my mind — never sit on committees. However, I am very glad that that other poet was not on the committee that awarded Yeats the Nobel Prize; otherwise it might have gone into less deserving hands.

Some time after this I was at another fashionable drawing-room, where I read for an hour, and was the only reader. On that occasion the War benefited, I believe, to the extent of a hundred pounds. At the end of the reading, I was approached by a tall, graceful old lady, who introduced herself as Lady Ritchie. I was so charmed with her that I accepted at once an invitation to lunch with her on the following day: although I did not know that she was Thackeray's daughter, or that Thackeray ever had any daughters, for that matter; and I was certainly not influenced by her being a lady of title. I accepted the invitation because of a wonderful charm in her voice and manner which did not seem to belong to the present age – and in spite of my dislike of these social engagements.

When I was there on the following day it seemed a strange, old-fashioned little world that I had dis-covered. I was at the house Thackeray's daugh-ter and I met there one of Dickens's daughters too. And it was strange indeed to hear Lady Ritchie talking so naturally of Tennyson and Browning, and other Victorians, without any reference at all to the living writers whom I was there to represent. It was quite obvious that Lady Ritchie knew nothing of my work, and her only interest in me came from two things. First, I had impressed her as a reader of poetry. Secondly, she was delighted to meet an author for the first time in her life who had actually worked with his own hands; from necessity, and not with the object of writing a book. 'And you,' she said, looking at me with wonder and interest, 'you have actually worked with your own hands for a living, like the common men we meet in the street. How extraordinary!'

I could have said that I had always done my best to avoid doing that and had only done so when forced by circumstances, and that I was far from being proud of what I had done in that way — but I did not like to destroy Lady Ritchie's world of wonder.

After lunch, when we were talking, just before I left, Lady Ritchie showed me a portrait drawing of herself, done by a master. Now the first thing I had noticed in Lady Ritchie was this — that she had a sweet, simple smile that never seemed to leave her face. It was one of those smiles that a woman sometimes retains all through her life, which is unaffected by wrinkles, false teeth or shrunken flesh. This smile was the very first

136

thing that I had noticed in her, and it was the only thing that I was to remember. The portrait was done when she was a girl of seventeen, I believe, and when I looked I saw to my astonishment that the portrait was as much like the woman of seventy as it was of the girl of seventeen. It was the smile that mattered, and we could not think of age, whether we looked at the woman herself or at her portrait.

These readings soon led to others of a different kind, where one or two poets would be invited to dinner and, when the dinner was over, others would come in until there was a large party. At last I began to think I was being used as a public entertainer, and came to the conclusion that I could be better employed at home in writing new poems instead of reading old ones for the pleasure of others. However, I was not justified in this, for wherever I went other people, as well as poets, tried to do something themselves to make the party successful. For instance, at one of these houses Lord Crewe took the floor and tried to remember and recite a poem he had written in his youth, but without much success.

Up to the present I have only dealt with literary

men, for I did not meet many artists and painters until later in my life. But to give this book some variety, I will finish my chapters on literary men by mentioning Arnold Bennett and Arthur Symons, although I did not meet them until after the War. These two writers were the last literary men of consequence that I have met; while St. John Adcock was the first, closely followed by Edward Thomas.

The first time I met Adcock I judged him to be a very young man; and when he began to talk of his children I came to the conclusion that he would not have many, and that they would be young and small. So when I paid him a visit on the following day, I had my pockets full of penny toys — a monkey on a stick, a couple of tin trumpets and a penny whistle. But when the first child came in I saw to my alarm that she was a young woman of sixteen or seventeen years of age; and even her younger sister, who came after, was far too big and old to welcome my toys. So I said nothing about them, and gave the toys to some poor children whom I met on my way back home.

The first thing I did on meeting Arnold Bennett, was to thank him for the early encouragement he had given to my work when he used to write reviews under the name of 'Jacob Tonson,' in his own early days of journalism. This was a splendid introduction, and we were soon at ease, sitting side by side and well pleased with each other's company.

'Whatever I have said as Jacob Tonson,' said Arnold Bennett, 'you are at liberty to repeat under the name of Arnold Bennett. Tell your publisher that.'

But while we were talking in this way, the gong, which we had not heard, had gone for dinner, and people were waiting for us to move into the dining-room. So we had to be reminded. Strange to say, nothing went right after that, and I began to see that Arnold Bennett was not the same man in a mixed crowd as he had been when we were together. For when I said something at dinner in praise of a certain play, he said emphatically – 'I don't agree with you, Davies, the thing is bad.'

Hearing this I waited, of course, to hear him give some reason, but to my surprise, he said again, after a long pause – 'the thing is bad.'

Still giving him another chance, I waited again

and, after a second long pause, out came the same words – 'the thing is bad.'

Now if he had only increased his vehemence, such as – 'the thing is bad, the thing is rotten, the thing is damn bad' – if he had only done this, I would have felt much less disappointed.

My first meeting with Arthur Symons, at the beginning of my literary career, had to be postponed owing to his serious illness, which lasted for years. And although I have met him since, I prefer to think of the man in his full powers, when he was the greatest critic of his day. I shall never forget how his one voice silenced all our literary Professors when they were comparing Stephen Phillips to Shakespeare and Marlow, and the way he did it, too ! Not by quoting the poet at his worst, but by taking the very passages that those professors were raving about, and showing that they were little better than rhetoric.

To be praised by Arthur Symons in those days meant the favour of the whole Press, which I was not long in finding out. His words were quoted everywhere, and every journalist I came in contact with told me of my good fortune in being praised by Arthur Symons.

This life in London — what a waste
   Of time and comfort, in this place;
With all its noise, and nothing seen
   But what is stone or human face.
Twigs thin and bare, like sparrows' legs,
   Yet back to Nature I must go —
To see the thin, mosquito flakes
   Grow into moths of plumper snow.

What is this life if, like bad clocks,
   We keep no time and are but going;
What is my breath worth when I hear
   A hundred horns and whistles blowing.
The rushing cars that crunch their way,
   Still followed by the heavy carts;
Till I, with all my senses stunned,
   Am deafened to my very thoughts.

*

It was winter now, yet for all that my thoughts went back to a quiet life in the country, although I knew that there were no flowers, and no birds singing, and the trees were bare. I was now getting tired of meeting people day after day, but there was no escape, for the Great War had now fastened every individual down to one place, where he was rationed for the necessities of life. Not only that, but it was impossible to find either a single room or a small house to let; and the only way to get a house was to buy it, and it needed money to do that. There were plenty of houses to be sold, but none to be let. Under these conditions, there was nothing to do but to make the best of life in London, and wait until the end of the War gave me freedom to go where I liked.

My readings for charity had now led me into another kind of life, where I met some interesting people. One of the most brilliant hostesses was Lady Cunard, whose luncheons were often attended by the Prime Minister and his family, by Balfour and others.

Lady Cunard was so straightforward that I took to her at once, for I knew that she would have no fear of saying to my face the things she would say behind my back. She was brilliant and witty and had a delightful way of misplacing her words, as when she spoke of the *unrivalled* ignorance of the Prime Minister, or the *irreproachable* imbecility of the House of Lords.

This is the strange way in which Lady Cunard

142

introduced three poets to a new-comer, when we stood talking together before lunch. 'This is Mr. A — —, who is a poet; this is Mr. Davies, *the* poet; and this is Mr. C — —, who also writes verses.'

People who know what this lady was doing at that time to help Opera, to make the name of a young and unknown artist, and to help literary men who were poor – people who knew these things would see nothing unkind in this.

Just as we sat down to lunch, Balfour came in, straight from affairs of State, and took a seat next to the hostess, nodding at one or two people he knew.

'That man there,' said Lady Cunard, dramatically, and pointing me out with her finger, – 'is W. H. Davies, the poet. He writes beautiful poetry, and his prose book, *The Autobiography of a Super-tramp* –' But when Lady Cunard got as far as this, Balfour exclaimed, almost impatiently – 'Don't talk to me of the work of Davies, for I know it far better than you do.'

Soon after this Lady Cunard was talking of 'the curious lack of intellect in the House of Lords.' To which Balfour answered that the House of

143

Lords contained more intellect than the House of Commons, but had less force to apply it.

This was followed by a discussion about the Law of Divorce, which one of the party said was made too difficult. 'No,' said another of the party, 'it is not that divorce should be made more easy, but that marriage should be made more difficult.'

When it came to this Lady Cunard, to my confusion, asked me loudly and personally for my opinion, and drew all eyes towards me. But I was so long in thinking of the matter, that another person relieved me of the responsibility, and said something else. If they had only waited another second or two I was going to say — 'The whole problem is easily solved by making it impossible,' which would have given them all a little amusement.

Probably the greatest moment of that hour, to me at least, was when Balfour was speaking of his former position as Prime Minister, and referred to it as 'before my fall.' When he used these three simple little words, it seemed to me to be the utterance of a god, and not a man. It seemed to me to be the one big moment, and strangely out of place among those efforts at wit which I admit were mostly successful.

Some time after this I heard Sir Robert Horne tell a rather good story, in which Balfour's singular and unique way of looking at things makes his wit a thing of its own, and entirely different from other people's. At that time there was a certain dance being performed, which some people thought to be too bold and immodest for a civilized country like England. As it was causing a great sensation, and was being discussed very earnestly by religious people, some members of the Cabinet thought in the interest of the State, that they would go and see the dance for themselves. When they had seen it, and the dance was over, they each gave his own opinion, one saying that the dance was disgraceful, another that it was a little immodest, but could be much worse, etc. Balfour was the last to speak, and they all stood waiting to hear his opinion. 'All I can see,' said Balfour, 'is this – one person seems to be trying to impede the progress of one of the opposite sex.'

My fame as a reader of poetry had now spread into all the fashionable houses of London, but

I knew what I was doing; and stood ready at any moment to call a halt. I was treated so well at these houses that I never once had cause to complain. What consoled me was the thought that if I stayed at home I would not, under the present conditions of war, be able to do any mental work.

On another occasion I was at a party given by Lady Randolph Churchill, of which Colonel Repington has written in his *Reminiscences*. I have been told, but have not read his book, that he introduces me as a poet who told a story about a cat, which no one appeared to understand or to be interested in. Now the truth of the matter is this — the story was certainly understood and caused a great amount of interest. Probably Colonel Repington, in writing his book, did not remember it and, having introduced my name as one of the party, had to say something about me. However, he has now left the story for my own telling, and I am grateful to him for leaving me this fresh material for my own book. This is the story of the cat.

The night before this party, when I had been lying in bed, I had jumped up suddenly, under the impression that a cat, or some other large animal, had leapt on my breast. But after I had thrown it off with my two arms, and had not heard its body fall on the floor, I came to the conclusion that I had been dreaming, although I could almost swear that I was awake. On the following morning a friend, who lived in the rooms above, came in to see me, and said – 'I hope I did not disturb you when I came in late last night.'

'No,' I answered, 'I did not hear you.'

'It is likely,' he continued, 'that I saved you from having a bad time; for when I reached your landing I found a large cat lying on the rug outside your bedroom door. So I took it down stairs, and gave it a chance to go to its own home.'

This was the story, with my comment that I thought that that cat had the power to make its presence known behind my locked door, without my having the least suspicion that it was there. The story is quite simple and caused some interest. I have never been known to be vague either in my work or conversation; and my meaning has never been lost in too many words; and that is why I cannot understand why Colonel

147

Repington did not remember it. Perhaps it was because he had had no more idea of writing a book at that time than I had. However, I must say that the best thing that was said after lunch, and the only thing I can remember, came from Colonel Repington himself, when he startled some of the ladies present by saying firmly and distinctly – 'I have found men to be far more innocent than women.' When they heard this, it was quite obvious that some of the ladies who were present had a hard look; and it was quite clear that even a poet talking about a cat was much pleasanter to listen to.

But although I may forget Colonel Repington's remark, and also my own story of the cat, I shall never forget the charming little ceremony at the end of the meal, and which I had not expected. It was when a servant brought in a large plate of broken bread, and stood standing there until Lady Randolph was ready to leave the table. When this bread arrived, I was considerably alarmed, for I had an idea that it played some part in our own meal, which apparently was over. So I made up my mind that if others refused the crumbs, so would I – in case I committed a breach

148

of good manners. However, my suspense was soon over, for as soon as Lady Randolph Churchill was on her feet, she led the way into the garden, closely followed by the plate of crumbs. Taking the bread in her own hands, she then distributed it for the pigeons and sparrows, that were already in waiting. After this charming little ceremony, we all made our way to the drawing-room, while I lingered in the rear to see the first birds picking at the soft, white bread.

It will be seen from this that my experience in another kind of life from the one I had been used to was far from unpleasant. If anything could be said against it, the fault was entirely my own; it was because of my shyness, which often made it painful for me to meet more than two or three people at a time. On one or two occasions this has taken the form of panic and fright, and I have actually left people's houses without wishing anyone good-bye. On one occasion, when I was due to read for some charity at Leighton House, my courage failed me at the very door, and I returned home immediately. I then wrote a note of apology, saying that I could not find the place.

At another time, when I was standing at the

door, waiting for a favourable opportunity to open it and slip away without being seen, the door was suddenly opened by a well-known lady journalist, whom I did not know at that time. Seeing the door opened suddenly, the host had stepped forward quickly and introduced us. The lady seemed pleased to meet me and led the way to a couple of chairs, so that we could talk in comfort.

But she had no sooner turned her back than I, seeing the open door, slipped out and never returned. What she thought of this conduct, which looked very much like an insult, as though I did not want to have anything to do with her — I cannot say. Yes, I can: she thought it so ungentlemanly and rude that since then I have been able to trace her displeasure in the Press — unsigned — of course. What a pity she did not know the truth, especially as my conduct gave her so much pain. For when I slipped away I was bored with so many people in one small room, the bad air, and the impossibility of talking to a French poet who knew as little English as I knew French — and was not thinking of her at all.

In speaking of this French poet, I am reminded of the one and only cruel joke I have ever played in my whole life. It was when a young foreigner asked me if I knew the address of one of our greatest poets, to whom he was writing.

'The address is Boar's Hill, Oxford,' I answered.

'How do you spell it,' asked the young foreigner, taking out his pen and note-book.

'B-o-r-e-s,' I answered, laughing to myself. For I was thinking of the great number of young poets who had taken rooms in or around Oxford so as to be near their masters; and I imagined them meeting and reading their own verses to each other. So I told him to write 'Bores' Hill, without having any disrespect for the one or two good poets who were then either living in or around Oxford.

In writing this book I had intended not to mention any of the younger men, and to confine myself to established names. But I must make an exception of one young poet, because it was the sensation of his death that set half the world writing poetry and the other half reading it. This young poet was Rupert Brooke who, through his great personal charm and his own personal connections, made his death the most extraordinary thing in the history of literature. He was made to represent Literature in the Great War; and his early death proved he had so many friends that, had he lived, he would have needed super-human strength to have made himself a great poet. If Rupert Brooke had not died, it is hardly likely that poets would have been asked to read their work to the public and that the interest in them would have been so great that people paid guineas to see and hear them.

To be honest and sincere, I must say certain things now that a good many people will not like. First of all, Rupert Brooke was not only not a great poet — his work shows not the least sign that he would ever have become one. For instance, all our great poets achieved greatness in their early work, either in passages or single poems, which they could never surpass in after years. Look at the fine things in 'Endymion.' And what of Shakespeare's sonnets, the first songs of Burns and the early poems of Milton? The only difference between their early work and their later was that their greatness was more sustained and they had less failures. But there is not the least sign in the work of Rupert Brooke to justify us in saying he would have become the first poet of his age, above Hardy, Yeats and Bridges. No, we must look on the death of Rupert Brooke as the passing away of a charming and a gay young spirit; and to talk of a severe loss to English poetry is all sentimental cant and humbug. Even his sonnet, which has been quoted as his best piece, 'If I should die' – even this is not very great as poetry; but seeing that he *did* die, it takes the significance of a prophecy and upsets our judgment. Not only that, but it is peculiarly dramatic and suitable for recitation, and, coming from a rich, fluent tongue, sounds large and impressive.

On one occasion, when I was dining out, a young writer came up to my table, and said— 'Have you heard the latest news?'

'What is it?' I asked, judging that it would have something to do with Literature.

'Rupert Brooke the poet,' said the young writer, 'has committed suicide in the Pacific, and is now a journalist.'

He was referring, of course, to Rupert Brooke's articles, describing his travels, which were being published in the *Saturday Westminster Gazette*, and which were not of much value as literature.

After saying these things, judging Rupert Brooke as a poet and man of letters, I will now come to him as a man, and in this I have nothing but praise. When I heard the news of his early death, it came to me as the first great blow of the War. The second blow came on the death of Edward Thomas, my first and oldest literary friend.

I met Rupert Brooke about a dozen times, I believe, and was always struck by his sound common-sense and his strong sense of humour. And, seeing that he looked up to me as a kind of master, I took full advantage of that fact and gave him what I thought was good advice. For instance, I knew that he was seeing too many people, so I preached the gospel of work. He always agreed to this, being well aware of that danger; and always said that he was going away to a quiet place almost immediately. On one occasion when he had repeatedly mentioned the name of a certain great lady and her views on different matters, I told him that it might be necessary — if he was to become a great author — to hear the opinions of Matilda Jane Ann and

Doll Tearsheet as well, which he would probably find interesting. He was not accustomed to this straightforward talk, but seemed thoroughly to enjoy it.

One morning he called at my house, on the chance of finding me at home and free to go out to lunch. So we went to a small restaurant in Soho, where he was to meet another friend. All I can remember of that lunch was this – the three of us did nothing but laugh all the time. Rupert Brooke and his friend were brimming over with gaiety, like two schoolboys. He was so boyish in his happiness that I had an impression that he had been saving his money for a month or more, and was now determined to spend every penny of it on food, drink, and rides. And that is how I like to remember him, wishing me good-bye and standing in his bare head, for he had come out without either a hat or a cap. Soon after that I heard the news of his death.

If this charming young man had lived, he might have become a good critic, even a great one, for he had excellent taste in poetry; but a greater poet than Hardy, Yeats, or Bridges – there is not the least sign of that.

WHEN I went wandering far from home,
I left a woman in my room
To clean my hearth and floor, and dust
My shelves and pictures, books and bust.

When I came back a welcome glow
Burned in her eyes — her voice was low;
And every thing was in its place,
As clean and bright as her own face.

But when I looked more closely there,
The dust was on my dark, bronze hair;
The nose and eyebrows too were white —
And yet the lips were clean and bright.

The years have gone, and so has she,
But still the truth remains with me —
How that hard mouth was once kept clean
By living lips that kissed unseen.

*

MY first meeting with artists was at a reception
given every Tuesday night at a lady's house
in Frith Street, Soho; where I was taken by a
clever and popular young intellectual, who was
doing all he could to get interesting people together. It was mostly for artists, and not so

much for literary people. Not only that, but the
artists were all revolutionaries who worked in their
own way without troubling themselves much about
the general public. To be popular was to be
damned, which I soon had cause to know. For
I soon heard one lady say to another — 'That's
W. H. Davies, the poet.' 'Oh, yes,' answered
the other lady with a sniff of scorn, 'we see his
name everywhere.'

Why are people always insisting that I am a
popular poet, which I certainly do not want to
be. If they want to know the truth, they only
have to count my editions.

Among the people at this gathering was that
extraordinary young genius, Bresco, the sculptor,
who was another victim of the Great War; and
who was probably the only living sculptor whom
Epstein took very seriously. Epstein was there
too; so was Sickert, and a number of younger
men, with or without reputations.

This was the first time I had met Sickert, and
I was very fortunate in finding that he knew my
work and was favourable towards it. I don't
know what started the discussion; but in less
than a minute after our introduction, Sickert

was saying how strange and unfair it was that there was Government assistance for men of letters and scientists, and none for artists. Sickert was saying this in his usual charming manner, for he himself had no cause to be bitter on that score, seeing that he did not need assistance of that kind. Now it had happened, strangely enough, that Edward Garnett had that very day turned to Hudson, Norman Douglas and other literary men, and said – 'If Davies had the same reputation as an artist as he has as a poet, he would be now making £5,000 a year, instead of a paltry £50, and sometimes less.'

This I repeated to Sickert, and added – 'If an artist is recognized his work sells for a good price, and he needs no help from the Government; but a poet can be recognized, and still not be able to make a decent living.'

After saying this I gave an instance of how John could do a drawing in an hour and get £40 or £50 for it; and that a lyric by Yeats, which would equal John's as a work of art, would fetch only two or three guineas.

Sickert appeared deeply interested in this, and

said that he had never looked on it in that way before. However, he mentioned one thing to prove that I myself had not seen every side of the matter. It was this – the artist had to have a studio, to hire models, to buy canvas, brushes and paint, etc.; whereas a poet could do his best work in any small place, and two pennyworth of paper and a penny bottle of ink would last him a year.

Sickert expressed the greatest astonishment when I told him that I had just received ten shillings and sixpence for one of my lyrics, and that there was only one paper that paid me as high as two guineas.

Some time after this I sat to Epstein for a bust on condition that he would give me one of the six bronze casts, and only charge me for the metal, which was very dear at that time. Epstein generously agreed to this, and said that I could have one for £10, which, of course, was worth from sixty to a hundred guineas. Now when I had this fine bronze bust in my possession, I was suddenly seized with an avaricious spirit to possess beautiful works of art, and wanted a John, a Sickert and others to go with it. As I had no money worth speaking about, the only thing to do was to sit for those artists, and – not being a paid and professional model – receive one of their pictures as a gift. But if they had no desire or interest to draw or paint me, how could it be done?

One morning, when I was passing a shop in Holborn, I saw a very small water-colour drawing by Sickert, which the shopkeeper told me was worth £15. But although I only had about £30 in the bank at that time, and needed clothes too, I was determined to possess a Sickert as soon as possible. The only thing that worried me was that the work might not have been genuine, seeing that the window contained so much other work that was all rubbish. So I thought it advisable to see Sickert first and ask him if he remembered doing the sketch – in case I wasted my money on a forgery. But when I saw Sickert and mentioned the matter, he began, instead of saying anything about the drawing in question, to expostulate in this way – 'Nonsense, poets can't afford to buy the works of artists. The best thing to do is for us to make each other presents of our own work. You give me some of your books, and I'll give you a picture.'

'But my books will only be worth two or three pounds,' I said, 'even though there are more than a dozen and they are all signed; while your picture will be of much greater value.'

But Sickert would not see the matter in this way, and in less than five minutes he had stood six paintings all in a row, to let me make my choice. This was rather difficult, but I surprised Sickert in the end by choosing what he himself had always thought to be one of the finest things he had ever done.

Sickert was surprised, but I could have told him of an incident that would have surprised him more. For one day, when I had looked into a shop window, I saw a picture of still-life, the subject being some apples on a table. 'If I had that picture,' thought I, 'I would never be without apples again; and I would have no more need to worry about their price, their season or crops.'

Looking at those apples a little closer, I was so taken with the richness of their painting that I was prepared to give half my fortune to possess them; which meant that I would give £10, my fortune at that time being £20. But I did not go into the shop for two reasons. First, I thought the picture would be too much for my purse, and I did not like the idea of raising the shop-keeper's hopes that I was going to buy it, and then coming out of his shop without spending a penny. The second reason was this – I always like to spend my money as though I am worth plenty more, and did not want the shopkeeper to think that I was too poor to pay the price he asked for his picture. This picture was by Fantin. Now, as I had never heard of such an artist – although I know now that he was one of the Masters – and judged it solely on its merit, it must be seen from this that I know somehow a good work of art when I see one.

This generosity of Sickert's was amazing, in spite of his statement that in reading my work he had been helped in doing his own. For he also gave me six etchings, all of which are to be seen on my walls.

Sickert was one of the most charming and wittiest men I have ever known. No matter what the subject was, he always found something witty to say about it. When he proposed going to

France with his wife, the journey had to be delayed for several days, owing to Sickert's fondness for a joke. For when he filled in the form of description, and came to the question of his wife's complexion, he wrote – 'charming and most delicious,' and when he had to describe the colour of her eyes, he wrote the word, 'heavenly,' This form was returned to him, of course, and he had to fill in another.

Sickert's success as a story teller is no doubt due to his having been on the stage for a short time in his early days; which gave him the power – although he did not have either a sweet or a rich voice – of being clear, emphatic and eloquent. For instance, the following story may not read very exciting, but to hear Sickert say it and see him act it, would be a different matter. I had commented on seeing four pictures of his, and all on the same subject. 'Yes,' said Sickert, 'that is the way I often work. First I do one picture and, when it is finished, I put it aside and say, "God." Then I do a second picture, which is a little better, and when I put that on one side, I say "God save." After that I do a third picture, still on the same subject. When that is done, I say "God save the." And now I come to the fourth picture, which has all the qualities I have been working for. When I put that picture down, the subject has grown to such a perfection that I can shout at the top of my voice – "God Save the King!" '

I once heard an artist say that critics favoured Sickert because they feared him, knowing that he had a biting wit, and a strong pen to strike back. I should think there was something in this statement, for it is just the same in literature. When editors or well-known journalists write books, they always have the entire favour of the Press; the abuse is kept back for the more solitary man of genius and the quiet dreamer. I shall be attacked for saying this, but no matter; for I would rather write another merry song than waste my time and temper on critics.

Sickert was an early riser and liked to cook his own breakfast in his studio, and share it with one or two others, before he started to work. He lived at Camden Town, I believe, but his studio was in Charlotte Street. So he proposed that I should join him at breakfast once a week, on Friday mornings. I did this for several months, and he made a few sketches of me, with the object of doing an engraving, but he did not appear to be satisfied that he was getting the best result. But when I went one Friday morning, I could get no answer to my knock, and left without seeing him. That night he came along and apologized, saying that he was in the studio all the time and heard my knock, but, forgetting that it was Friday, and my morning, was afraid to answer the door to anyone else. This ended our breakfasts, for the following week he was going to Dieppe, where he had a house, and did not know when he would return to England.

While I am writing of Sickert, I must mention one of his best friends, Harold Gilman, of whom I once saw a great deal, because we used the same haunts. Gilman called to see me quite a number of times, and every time he came he criticized a certain portrait of mine which, I must admit, was feeble in every way. Gilman hated it, and every time he saw it wanted me to sit to him for a portrait to show how much better it could be done. But as he was then in an experimental stage, and had strange ideas of colour, I thought I would wait — on the advice of a friend — until his ideas became more settled. For I did not want Gilman to paint my face bloated and purple, like the face of a drowned man who has been found after many days in the water.

One night, when I was sleeping on my couch in the front room, so as to be better able to hear if there should be an air-raid — this picture fell off the wall and almost stunned me. The very first words I heard on the following morning were these — 'Harold Gilman has died suddenly of influenza.'

Now as there had never been any other than friendly feeling between Gilman and myself, I could only account for this in one way. That in his delirium, when dying, he was thinking of that portrait which he had so much detested; and, in his imagination, had struck it off the wall. But the connection between these two facts — the imagination of a dying artist and the solid substance of a real picture — is left for others to explain or to suggest some meaning.

I have already mentioned sitting to Epstein for a bust. This was before the War became so serious that the age-limit had to be raised to fifty years.

The Tribunals were not only brutal, but often ignorant men. This is what they said to Epstein — 'you have made a great name as a sculptor, and we are going to give you a chance now to make a name as a soldier.'

Epstein was a man of few words, but there was always strong matter behind them. On one occasion, when I asked him what he thought of a certain picture in the Academy, done by a contemporary, he simply shrugged his shoulders and said — 'It is one of the horrors of the War.'

And when I told him about a certain one-armed artist, whose work impressed me as being very clever, Epstein answered astutely — 'If you had told me that you had met a very clever artist, I could have believed you; but when you say he has only one arm, I must have my doubts about his cleverness.'

When I heard this I was brought at once to a better understanding, and knew that I had been under the influence of sentiment. For of course an artist only works with one hand after all; and if he had a hundred arms his work would be none the better.

As I am not an art critic, I will say nothing of

what I think of Epstein's work. But I would like to say that nothing I have ever seen before, in the world of dead matter, has given me more delight than the small head of a baby, which I once saw at one of the galleries. There it was, with its little, open mouth, pleading – as I heard a lady say maliciously – for sixty guineas. However, she meant no harm by this, and was only annoyed that she was not rich enough to possess it. If I had been a rich man, that baby's face would not have pleaded in vain, even for twice that amount.

I got on very well with Epstein, as I always do with Jews, or, for that matter, anyone else. But it was quite obvious to me, right at the beginning, that he had a mind that was easily poisoned by other people, and what he needed, more than any other man I had ever met, was a good friend to tell him that he did not have as many enemies as he believed. However, he was not suspicious of me, and I already had the good opinion of most of his friends.

When I sat for Epstein he had just bought a large, strange-looking figure, which he had found in a second-hand shop and bought for a few shillings. He had thought, right at the beginning, that the thing was very old and of great value; and when he had brought it home and examined it more thoroughly, he was positive that that was the case, and made up his mind to sell it to the British Museum. 'Now,' said Epstein, 'the British Government has always been mean in buying works of art, and when they take this they will have to pay me a good price for it. What sum do you think I ought to sell it for, Davies?'

'I wouldn't take a penny less than £2,000,' I answered.

'We will see,' said Epstein. 'I may let it go for less, but don't know yet.'

Not long after this Epstein was called out of the room, to see three representatives from the British Museum, who had come to examine a great treasure and make an offer for it.

In about a quarter of an hour they had gone and Epstein returned to the studio, looking sad and disappointed.

'They have not persuaded you to sell it for two or three hundred pounds, I hope,' I began to say, with some alarm.

'No,' answered Epstein, ' but what they said was this — "it was a splendid thing as a copy, but there were certain signs to show that it was not old and genuine, and was only an imitation. It was worth," they said, " about ten or twelve shillings." '

'But surely,' I said, 'you are not going to take their word for it, are you? Why can't they make a mistake?'

'Of course, they have made a mistake,' answered Epstein, his old confidence returning to him.

When I left Epstein I was very pleased to see that he was still as confident as the cannibal in the story. Do you know the story of the cannibal who was brought into court to serve as a witness? When the judge said — 'There is nothing to prove the death of John Summers, no grave, no stone and no monument, this cannibal pointed to his own round belly, and exclaimed proudly — "I am the grave! I am the stone! I am the monument!" '

Some time after these meetings with Sickert and Epstein, I had been invited to spend a few days with William Rothenstein, down in Gloucestershire. He wanted to do a portrait of me, and said that he would not have asked me to make so long a journey had he not thought I would enjoy the change of air and different scenery.

When I reached him, I found that he was spending all his mornings in painting one tree, which stood all alone in a meadow.

His studio was full of this tree, seen under different conditions of light and in different seasons. The position of that fine tree was so solitary and unique in being planted right in the centre of a large green meadow – that I could quite understand the fascination to the mind of an artist. And when I think of some of his fine studies of it, I always feel sorry that Rothenstein had never made me a little present of his work, for sitting to him – as every other artist had done, from John, Epstein, Sickert, Nicholson, Laura Knight, down to a number of younger artists who are not so well known. Rothenstein is the one name I miss on my walls in spite of sitting to him for portraits on two different occasions.

In the afternoon Rothenstein spent his time in working at a large oil portrait of himself. Now Rothenstein is certainly no better looking than I am. I have a distinct recollection of my grandmother saying to me once – 'you are ugly enough to please any woman, no matter how particular she might be.'

So when I saw Rothenstein standing there, with a large fat smile on his lips, as he painted himself by looking into a mirror – when I saw this I felt that I must either rush out of the room or strike him a heavy blow on the back of the head. However, Rothenstein's smile in the evening, when he sat with his three children, and was a father instead of an artist, was a different thing altogether.

The evenings were spent in Rothenstein reading the poems of Tagore, the Indian poet, whom he had drawn and painted a good many times. But although I offered a little criticism, Rothenstein did not mind in the least, but still went on reading.

Some time after this I met another great admirer of Tagore, who was a lady this time. 'I wonder,' said I, 'what Tagore, being an Indian, thinks of Kipling's fine stories of Indian life.'

'He would never think of him,' answered the lady in a lofty voice.

173

An artist draws his own strange mind,
  We're but his mirrors — I and you;
If he's a devil — so am I;
  If he's an angel — I'm one too.

*

Although I do not claim to have any great knowledge of art, yet for all that I have often been struck by one peculiarity — it is the touch of caricature which is employed by so many of our modern masters. When we see a portrait by an old master, we feel certain that it is a good likeness of the sitter, because it looks so natural, with no exaggeration. But some of our modern masters do not trouble much about a true likeness, and draw or paint a face in the way they themselves would like to see it. For that reason, we often see striking portraits that are not only unlike their subjects, but often wilfully misrepresent them. On one occasion a lady who admired my work, said, on seeing a portrait of me by a modern master — 'I would not like to meet the poet personally, because his mouth looks so hard and cruel.' She was surprised to hear from my publisher that far from having a face like that, I was always good-tempered and

175

smiling, and looked what I was – 'a poet of joy.'

One of the strangest criticisms I have ever heard, when speaking of portraits, came from the mouth of an illiterate window-cleaner, who had come to clean my windows. I had given that man some help time after time, although I was not much better off than he was. So you can judge of his annoyance when he first saw a certain portrait of me – just done by one of our modern masters – and what do you think he said? He did not say, pointing to the portrait, in which I was made to look cruel and hard-hearted – 'I would not like to meet that man,' because he already knew me as a good fellow. Instead of that, he said – 'The artist who did that portrait must have had a very evil spirit, and I would not like to know him.' People who did not know me, especially art-critics, would place their confidence in the artist, of course; and it would never once occur to them that the artist had no real truth of my work, my life and character.

On one occasion, when I allowed a young artist to do a portrait of me, he muttered something beneath his breath, and I just caught the words –

'find the beast.' Now, why be so particular to find the beast in a man when that man may have some other quality which is strong enough to keep the beast chained up so that it is never allowed to break loose and become wild?

Another artist, to whom I had offered a glass of wine, carefully arranged the bottle and glass on the table, and then did a portrait of me in which I was to be seen as a gaunt, sick wreck of a drunkard, who was in the act of drinking himself to death. He did this in spite of my broad shoulders, my round face and healthy looks. I may as well say here that the artist drank three glasses of wine to my one, which proved that he was not painting *my* character, but his own.

It is a strange contrast to see two great artists like Sickert and John at work. For Sickert never appears to be worried at the presence of others; but John, being a very silent man, could do nothing under those conditions. Sickert is a great lover of words, and even some of the titles of his pictures are works of art. For instance, one of the six pictures he showed me, to choose one for myself, was called – 'The Cow-Woman.' Now to call a woman a cow is the worst thing that could happen; and if his model, a woman of the lower classes, had only known that Sickert was calling her that, there would have been trouble indeed. He would have soon found himself confronted by a woman of ungovernable fury:

> As fierce as twenty angry cats,
> Rolled up and fighting in one ball.

It would have taken all Sickert's charm and eloquence to have persuaded that woman as to what he really meant – that the cow gave milk and she, being big, buxom and strong, looked as though she could have suckled twenty babies a day and still feel no ill-effect.

I have heard several people complain of John because of his terrible silence, and the way he goes on working and working, forgetful that his model needs a little rest occasionally.

When I sat to John for a portrait the work had been commissioned, but several people, not knowing this, wanted to buy it. But John did not even trouble to answer their letters and I – who also have a strange dislike to answering letters – was called upon to answer for the artist.

178

The result of the first day's sitting, when I had sat for several hours, was the most astonishing portrait I have ever seen; and I felt certain that it should have been left unfinished, because of its strange beauty. Some people would have said – 'Who ever saw a man look like that?' But I feel certain that John was right in his interpretation because of the strange thing that had happened, of which John knew nothing. For when I saw that the artist was an unusually silent man and, although he showed no signs that he was not interested in what I said, yet for all that went on with his work without answering by a single word – when I saw this I naturally fell into a silence of my own.

Now as I wanted to sit quite still and not change my position, so as to give the artist a fair chance, I had fixed my eyes on a little eye of light that came peeping through a curtain. 'If I keep my eyes on that little eye of light as a guide,' thought I, 'there will not be much fear of me changing my position.' But after I had been looking at that small light for about a quarter of an hour, it began to grow and advance into the room. And after I had been looking at it for twenty minutes it had come right into the centre of the room, and had grown from the size of a gooseberry to the size of an orange. I began to wonder what would happen to me when that light, still growing and advancing, reached my face. What would have happened I cannot tell, for I was suddenly brought to my senses by hearing some one tapping and, turning my eyes, saw John in the act of knocking the ashes out of his pipe. And when I looked again the light had gone.

I did not tell John anything of this experience, but I should think that my face must have made a very interesting study, and was the cause of the inspired look he had given it in his portrait. That I had almost hypnotized myself by looking so intently at that light is most certain.

After six days' hard work – six days in which John paid me the compliment of being a strict teetotaller – the portrait was done, and is now at Cardiff, in the National Gallery of Wales.

Some time after this John did a drawing of me, as a present for my trouble, which I was happy to add to my Epstein and Sickerts. But the drawing is so much unlike the oil painting that no one could trace the remotest resemblance between them. In the drawing I have fallen from my high seat in heaven, where John first placed me, and have become a very devil.

I have often heard it said how much John is admired and worshipped by his younger contemporaries, and on one or two occasions it has been brought home to me in an unusual way. I was sitting in the Café Royal on one occasion, and had my attention drawn to two young men who were looking around the place and commenting on other people. When they looked my way, I naturally turned my head in another direction, for they were too near to stare into their faces. One of them then said, looking at me, I suppose – 'That's Davies, the poet.' 'Oh, yes,' answered the other – 'he's a John, isn't he?' When I heard this I was not very well pleased, to think I was only a John and nothing more. However, my satisfaction came almost immediately, for in the young fellow's excitement to have a good look at me, he knocked over his glass of port. This piece of bad luck proved that I was something of a Jonah as well as a John.

At another time, still at the Café Royal, there was a fine example of the respect in which John is held by his many admirers. John had fallen asleep, tired, I suppose, after doing a day of hard, concentrated work. While he was sitting there, an admirer, just coming in from the street, went up to speak to him, not knowing that John was not well awake. On seeing this, another great admirer, who had taken up a position close to John, suddenly rose to his feet and, stretching out his arm to prevent the other from coming closer, said in an awed whisper – 'Hush! He sleeps.'

Certain pictures I have seen have always held a great fascination for me, because they have a mystery that I cannot understand. For instance, there is Sickert's picture, called 'Ennui,' in which we see a man seated with a woman's body across his left shoulder and his left arm around her waist. His right arm is occupied in smoking a cigar, and it is quite obvious that his mind is more interested in his right arm than his left. The woman, too, is bored, and her whole attitude seems to say – 'I may as well be here as anywhere else.' Now if an inferior artist had done that picture, he would have placed those two people far apart, the man either reading or sleeping, and the woman either sewing or looking out of the window. But

182

a great artist like Sickert can even join their bodies together, and still show that their minds have lost all interest in each other. How is it done? That is the master's secret.

Another picture of this kind is one by John, in which we see two common field-workers, who have paused in their work to take a hug of love. But it is a primitive love, the love of savages; for the man has planted himself so firmly, and holds her so strongly, that it looks as though he intended to throw her into eternity. It looks as much like murder as love. It is the love of our first blood — as mysterious as the voices of two cats when we cannot tell whether they are making love to each other or tearing each other to pieces. And yet we know, without being told, that it is a scene of love. How is it done? That again is the master's secret.

Another work of art that has had the same effect on me is Epstein's head of John. Now John has a massive head, and when his hair is long and he is bearded you will not meet many men who look more like a lion. But though John's head has this majesty about it, as it is seen in life, yet in Epstein's cast of it it looks puny and small. This, of course, could be understood if we measured the

two heads, the living and the dead, and found that
Epstein had reduced the dead head in size. But,
strange to say, all the dimensions are correct, and
the head is the same size in clay as it is in the
flesh; and though the dead head looks small, *it
is not small.* How is it done? It is the secret of a
master.

But these questions ought to be left to others,
for I am not an art critic; and in writing this book
I want to deal with persons and not their work.

It was not until towards the end of the Great
War that I met William Nicholson: and in not
knowing him before I missed a good fellow. He
was always full of good stories of people and
things, and had a clean tongue, too. If he told a
story that went against himself he appeared all
the happier. Such as when he paid a visit to a
great house in the country, and a servant was sent
to meet him. And how the servant was so un-
impressed by the new-comer's conversation that
he drove Nicholson to the servants' quarters at
the back of the house and was astonished to hear
that he was expected at the front door.

I remember, too, how happy Nicholson was on
another occasion, when he had gone out to get

some tobacco and I was waiting for him. For when he had reached the street corner he found some four or five minstrels getting ready to perform. But when these men saw Nicholson coming — dressed exactly like themselves, in a black coat and white trousers — they looked considerably angry and whispered together. All of them then set their eyes on Nicholson and waited until he had gone, thinking he had a tin whistle in his pocket or a banjo under his coat, and was a rival!

On another occasion Nicholson and I spent the whole evening in making schemes that were to astonish and alarm the whole population of London. One scheme was to get certain powders which, Nicholson said, could be had from a friend of his. We would then drop some of this powder in the water at Trafalgar Square, and it would soon be seen that the fountain was spouting blood. This would cause a tremendous sensation, which would be increased on the following day when, a different powder being used, the spouted water would be green or black. This scheme appeared so simple and so easy to perform, that I have often been surprised that we did not put it into practice and enjoy the sight of turning thousands of bored

185

and unexcited Londoners into country sightseers, and to listen to their puzzled tongues.

Another scheme was to wear rubber gloves with the palms smeared with fresh, red paint. We would then visit certain houses — mostly the houses of public men — and stamp a bloody hand on their front windows. This we could do night after night for a considerable time, without much fear of being caught red-handed. We would not be confined to one place, as we would when dropping powder into the water at Trafalgar Square; and, being free to change our locality, the mystery and wonder could go on for a month or more. And we could meet every day and read the papers, hearing what they had to say about 'The Mystery of the Bloody Hand.'

Nicholson has told me one story at least that has probably given me more delight than any other I have ever heard or read. It was about a well-known dramatist who got up for breakfast one morning feeling sick and without appetite, owing to a series of social engagements and their late hours. So, feeling in this delicate condition, he naturally did not give his breakfast a very encouraging look, when it was brought in by a man-

186

servant – although it was a dish of kidneys, a thing he had often relished when in a better state of health.

'You don't like the look of them, sir?' said the man in a voice of deep sympathy. 'Pardon me for speaking, sir, but neither do I. They always remind me of when I worked for a doctor and assisted him at an operation to remove the kidneys from a coloured gentleman!' Needless to say, the dramatist did not have any breakfast at all on that particular morning.

One morning Nicholson drove up to my place in a taxicab in a great hurry. It was to invite me to a dinner he was giving that night before he went abroad. With my usual shyness, I asked him how large the party was to be, and heard, to my relief, that it would only consist of himself, his wife and Fanny Pryde – all known to me – and possibly one other.

Nicholson always apologized for taking a taxi-cab and paying two shillings for it, by saying that he was too poor to take a 'bus and pay twopence. He meant, of course, that he had to make the best use of his time, so as to keep up a position in life. For instance, it paid him better if he had an engagement at four o'clock, to keep on at his work until 3.45, and then pay a taximan two shillings for a quick journey – rather than to stop working at 3 o'clock and then pay a 'bus conductor twopence for a slow journey.

When I arrived for dinner that evening I found on entering the room that nearly all the party was known to me, and it was only necessary to introduce me to one man, who was Max Beerbohm.

Now when I saw that little and small great man standing there, dressed perfectly in the white and black of evening dress, I thought he was, as a man, the most harmless and gentle creature I had ever seen; the kind of man who would go through life with his eyes on the ground, to give worms their right to cross his path. And when I heard his quiet little voice – full of small hesitations and stammers – this idea impressed me more than ever. However, it was not long before I found that Max not only had something to say, but could say it with some force too. What I mean is this – he was just as powerful with his tongue as with his pen or pencil.

As soon as we were seated for dinner, some one raised the question of an attack on Shaw, which had just been written by one of the younger generation. The only thing that could be said in favour of that young writer was that he was ill and suffering from the severe strain of the war, and had lost all reverence for a man who was not only greater than he would ever be, but was also old enough to be his father. This was the opinion I expressed at the dinner party. But Max objected to my words at once, for he did not like 'old enough to be his father.' 'For,' said he, 'there is no age in art; and it makes no difference whether the young attack the old, or the old or young attack each other.'

But it was not much good to continue this subject, because Max had not read the article, and looked on it as a clever work of art; whereas it was feeble, unpleasant and ill-natured.

Not only that, but I now began to see that Max was very exact and particular in the choice of words, and that though he might agree with one's opinion, it was not certain that he would agree to the way it was expressed.

A few years before this dinner I had met another man, an art critic, who was exactly like Max in this. He argued about nothing at all, just for the sake of making you express an opinion in the exact terms he would use himself. On one occasion, when this man had called at my place, he gave me one of his little books, which consisted of short stories and a few articles on Rembrandt and others. The first sentence I read, on opening his book, ran like this — 'It was eight o'clock exactly, and Marie, etc.' Exactly!

As soon as dinner was over, Max made his way toward me, and I advanced a step or two to meet him, without the least suspicion of what was to follow.

'How long is it since Shaw discovered you?' he asked, in a gentle voice.

Now when I heard this I felt at once that there was something wrong, and that I was being asked a question that would be dangerous to answer. The question reminded me of when I was asked by a certain woman — 'How much money have you got, coppers and all?'

However, the question called for an answer of some kind, so I said — 'About fourteen or fifteen years ago, I believe.'

'Oh dear, dear!' exclaimed Max, in an aggrieved voice. 'Oh dear, dear — and has it been going on all this time!' — implying, of course, that it was about time I was forgotten.

'Yes,' I answered, adopting the same serious and aggrieved tone — 'yes, and it is likely to go on much longer too' — implying that my name would not be forgotten for a long time to come.

This round went in my favour, I believe, but I will leave others to judge that.

The next moment Max began again in a gentle, soothing voice, and Nicholson had now drawn near, to hear what we were talking about.

'Shaw,' began Max, hesitating and stammering — 'Shaw saw at once that you were — a real poet; and — of course — being a decent fellow — like a good many more — just lent a hand — the same as most people — would have done — and — and helped a lame dog over the stile.'

Saying this he edged away quietly, and Nicholson, seeing that the battle was over, went off to speak to some one else. This blow knocked me out completely, for I *was* lame, and the expression was not figurative, as it would have been with others. There I stood dazed and half-stunned and wondering as to what had happened; in the same state as a man when he is washing, and the soap-suds in his ears are whistling like birds.

When I mentioned this incident to a friend, some time after, he said – 'Davies, you were hit below the belt and fouled. It was not a clean blow.' However, when I appealed to Nicholson, who was the referee of that last and second round, he says – 'No, I don't think so.' But perhaps he wants to be faithful to *two* friends, instead of one.

However, I soon recovered, and it was not long before I was seated at the side of Fanny Pryde, and talked with her for the rest of the evening. Once or twice I looked around to see what the other people were doing; and saw that Max was in a far corner poring over a book. But I don't know whether it was a printed book and he was reading, or a blank book in which he was making sketches of the company.

Max is a very clever man. Of all our living celebrities, his mind is the most subtle; and his knowledge of human nature is almost uncanny and diabolical. For instance, why did he go from place to place and speak of a certain actor in this way – 'What a pity it is that A——, who is such a nice fellow, should be such a bad actor!' Max knew, of course, that to call a man a nice fellow

192

is not worth repeating, as nice fellows are common, but to call a man a bad actor is to be sure that the words will be repeated everywhere. And if these words come to the ears of A——, what then? He would not give a pin for being called a nice fellow, but to be called a bad actor —

And why did Max call another man a Japanese Jew? Speaking for myself, I like Jews, as I have said before; and of all the coloured races, I certainly like the Japanese best. And yet, somehow the very thought of a Japanese Jew makes me think of freaks and abortions. I can no longer enjoy a little quiet laugh, as when I think of a Scotch Jew. Now if the thought of a Japanese Jew has this uncomfortable effect on me, who has no prejudice against either Jew or Japanese — what would the effect be on others who do not like either?

Nicholson has told me several good stories about Max, and in case they should be forgotten and never get into print, I would like to give one or two of them here, and to thank Max for so much good copy.

It will be remembered that, a few years ago, a shilling subscription was started throughout the country to make a presentation to Dr. Grace, the famous cricketer. To this Max contributed, like thousands of other Englishmen, and sent his little shilling, with a note to this effect — 'I send you this shilling, not because I am a great admirer of cricket, but as an earnest protest against golf!'

When an American lady, on being introduced to Max, began to say — 'I guess you are thought a lot of in England, Mr. Beerbohm,' Max answered quickly — 'Oh yes, yes, but I am in no immediate danger of being buried alive in Westminster Abbey.'

On another occasion, a lady, who was a great admirer of Max's work, expressed a wish to see his studio. Max had no studio, of course, for his work could be done anywhere — and this he told her. However, as she still insisted that the room he worked in would have a certain fascination for her, he relented and invited her for the following day. 'And may I bring a friend along with me?' asked the lady.

'Yes, yes,' answered Max in despair, 'you may as well — and kill one bird with two stones.'

Another story is of a lady who wished to read Max's horoscope. She had already been told the name of the place where he was born, also the year, the month, and even the day. At last she wanted to know the very hour, and it was now that Max failed completely. However, not wanting to spoil the horoscope at the last minute, he answered desperately – 'Oh, about the usual time!'

With this chapter I close my impressions of literary men and artists, and what follows is personal matter. If people are sufficiently interested, let them read on; but if they are not, they had better stop reading now, with the flavour of these stories in their mouths.

It will be seen that I have not disliked anyone who is to be found in this book, and everything I say is said without malice. Some of the men in this book were not met under fair conditions. Hudson, for instance, was a disappointed man, and was probably a much more genial companion in the years that followed, which brought him recognition in his old age. And when I met Conrad, the conditions were not fair then, for all his thoughts at that time were about his own country and countrymen. I do not trouble much what others think of me, for I have one peculiar gratification –

I have never, in all my life, expressed a wish to meet anyone; and when I have met people, it has never been of my own seeking.

I would like to say, too, that I am writing this book entirely from memory, and never had the remotest idea of writing about these people — until a few months ago.

How sordid is this crowded life, its spite
And envy, the unkindness brought to light:
It makes me think of those great modest hearts
That spend their quiet lives in lonely parts,
In deserts, hills and woods; and pass away
Judged by a few, or none, from day to day.
And O that I were free enough to dwell
In their great spaces for a while; until
The dream-like life of such a solitude
Has forced my tongue to cry 'Hallo!' aloud –
To make an echo from the silence give
My voice back with the knowledge that I live.

*

THE Great War was now over, and I had left my flat in Holborn and taken two small rooms in the West End. The nuisances I had to complain of in my flat were not entirely due to human beings, but to rats, which, for a short period, became a dangerous menace. To paraphrase the drunken sailor when, waking from sleep and finding his arm around a lamp post, he said, 'I have been in longitude, and I have been in latitude; but this is the first time I have ever found myself in this bloody attitude' – so I myself could say, 'I have been among rats on board ship, and I have been among rats in barns; but this is the first time I have ever been among them in a house.'

These rats used to come up the steps that led into a deep, dark cellar that was no longer used, owing to the shopkeeper having given up his right to it when he let the rooms above his shop. One night, when I reached home late, I had no sooner touched the front door with my key than I heard a terrible scuffle behind the door, like two men fighting. It was the rats that, seized with sudden panic, were eager to escape into the cellar, and were so numerous that they were in each others' way. So I had to wait a little while to give them every chance to get away.

On another occasion, when I was sitting before my fire and reading, there was such a loud bang at the door that I thought burglars were in the house and were trying to force the lock. But when I opened the door, there was not only no sign of any life at all, but there was not even the faintest sound of anything going away. I came to the conclusion that a big, heavy rat, desperate at being kept out of my room, had taken a running leap and thrown his body against the door, with the intention of bursting it open by sheer force.

At other times I could hear them on the stairs outside, sounding exactly like human beings, as they flopped from step to step in passing to and fro. The only thing that consoled me was the thought that they had not yet succeeded in getting into my rooms. However, I was soon to have a very disagreeable surprise, for one morning, when I opened my eyes, I found a small bone, fresh and bloody, lying close to my bed. And when I thought of the fearlessness and impudence of that rat, that he had brought his bone there to gnaw it right under my nose — when I thought of this, I began to think of more dangers to my throat than a tickling cough. But I had now found other rooms and was moving; and, although that rat had chuckled at his grim jest, and had told the story to a hundred others, where they reigned undisputed in their dark cellar, and had probably given them great amusement — it was certain that he would not have a chance to repeat it.

But I had not been living in the West End many weeks before I was suddenly struck down with rheumatism and fever, and had to take to my bed. I not only could not stand or walk, but even lost the entire use of my arms; and although

I recovered the use of my arms in a few days, it was over a month before I could get out of bed for my meals.

I was very fortunate at this time in having a good housekeeper; and to prove that this serious illness was not only a test of her good qualities as a nurse, but that it also proved her to be a woman of great sympathy and tenderness, whose thoughts were not altogether in my purse. As a young woman who had not been accustomed to many luxuries, it probably pleased her to share my delicacies. For instead of spending most of my money on ale and wine, as I had been doing up till then, I now had, in my delicate condition, to spend it on chicken, followed by peaches and cream. By doing this I was not only able to eat enough to keep myself alive, but I also had the pleasure of hearing a woman's voice grow softer and sweeter, like a bird that is grateful for rain.

One morning, when this woman was carefully arranging my pillow and smiling happily, I said – 'You seem to be so happy that I feel almost sorry to tell you that I am feeling much better.'

'I am very pleased to hear that,' she answered – 'but I am happy because I am now doing the work

I am well used to. I have done these things so often at home, beginning when I was a little child at school. Illness is no worry to me.'

Now although this woman had been with me for some time, I had never been curious to know much about her private life. Cases of this kind are common in a large city like London, where we come in contact with certain people every day, and still know very little about them. Although they are familiar to us in the sun, we have no idea where they are when the moon is up.

It was now, for the first time, that this woman began to tell me something of her own home and family, to which I listened with close attention. Her father, it seems, had been an invalid for a number of years before he died, and sometimes had to take to his bed for a month, and sometimes more. So that his wife often had to sit up all night to attend to his wants. This meant that there had to be another, to give the night-watcher a chance to sleep by day. And as the family were too poor to hire a nurse or outdoor assistance, and lived on a lonely farm, with no near neighbours — under these circumstances my housekeeper had to be called up for duty, even before her fourteenth year. Now when her father was not in pain, though lying helpless in bed, the child enjoyed herself very well indeed. For her father was a bigger and a much more wonderful doll than the little wax figure she used to love. She washed his hands and face, and dried them too. She combed his hair time after time, and made curls, which he seemed to enjoy as much as she did. The only time he became serious and cried out with alarm was when he saw her standing near the bed with a pair of scissors in her hand, ready to cut his hair. But in spite of all her coaxing, he still refused to give her permission to do that.

This had been my housekeeper's experience as a child, and I could now see the reason why it gave her so much joy to bathe my foot, to wash my hands and face, and to comb my hair.

While my housekeeper was telling me these interesting things, and thoroughly enjoying their recital, she was still combing my rebellious hair; which still refused to take any other shape than the one to which its master had trained it for many and many a year.

Things went on like this for about ten days, and then came the worst experience of my life – my

housekeeper, who had on several occasions complained of having pains, was suddenly struck
down herself, and had to be removed to a
hospital. If this could have been done at once,
the case would not have been so bad, and it would
have meant less suffering for the both of us.
Needless to say, all my sympathy went to the
poor creature in the room below me; and I was
filled with the horror of thinking she must die
without assistance.

It was a long time indeed before she could be
removed, and I had to lie there helpless in the
room above, listening to her groans and cries of
pain. These sounds became so loud and violent
at last that I could hear the people in the street
coming to a halt under her window, to listen.
One or two of them, at the risk of interfering in a
private matter, entered the shop and said to the
manageress – 'There is a woman here in great
pain; can nothing be done for her?'

The manageress then came up to my room, and
said, 'Your housekeeper is in a terrible state of
pain – shall I go for a doctor?'

But there was no doctor to be found – they were
out of town or visiting patients. Strange to say, it

203

had not once occurred to me to send for my own doctor; but when the manageress told me of her failure to find one, I mentioned the matter then. However, he too was not at home, and would not be back for an hour or more.

When he came at last, he succeeded in giving the woman temporary relief from pain, but said that she must go to the hospital immediately.

But at eight o'clock that night the woman was still lying in bed at my house. The manageress of the shop had been in communication with several hospitals, but none of them had accommodation.

When it was nearly nine o'clock the manageress came up to me again, and said – 'What are we to do?'

At last it was decided to go to the police station. But when the officer in charge had the case explained to him, he only nodded his head and said – 'It is not for the police to do this.' However, when the manageress was returning with this bad news, she spoke to a constable who was on duty near us and insisted on his entering the house and seeing the woman. He had no sooner done this than he came up to my room, and said – 'The woman looks dying, and something must be done at once. Now if I have the police ambulance sent along to remove her to a hospital, are you willing to pay the expenses, which will be a pound or more? It is a difficult case,' he continued, 'because she is inside a house. When we pick up a woman in the street, we generally manage to get her into a hospital in twenty minutes, and sometimes less.'

'We have made a great mistake,' I answered; 'for if this poor woman had been thrown into the gutter, or placed on some one's doorstep, she would have been in a hospital hours ago.'

'That's quite right, sir,' answered the policeman, as he left the room.

It was about half an hour before the ambulance came, and when my housekeeper was being carried downstairs, the clock at Westminster was striking the hour of eleven. This made it seven hours since she was taken ill, and she was not in the hospital yet!

Another unpleasant feature was this — the sight of a police ambulance standing at my front door caused fifty or sixty people to gather there; and as the public-houses had only just closed, more than half of them were the worse for drink, and did not know whether they witnessed a funeral or a wedding, and behaved accordingly.

But even after the ambulance had reached the hospital, there was still something to fear; for the poor woman was refused admittance, in spite of a letter from the doctor. And it was only after one of the hospital doctors had seen her and said it was a very serious case that she was allowed to be taken out of the ambulance.

The next morning, after my housekeeper had been removed to the hospital, a woman was sent up from the shop below, as I had to have some one to look after me. But it did not give me much pleasure to see an old slovenly woman standing there in the place of my late housekeeper. There was nothing now in the way of affection, and it was all a question of money; and she came and went at her appointed hours, studied to the very minute.

It was the presence of this woman that made me at last make every effort to recover my independence. One evening I sat on the side of my couch and reached out for my boots. But the left foot was so swollen that it was impossible to wear a boot, even in a loose state. However, I thought of my slippers, and with them I succeeded. But when I stood upright I had no more idea of walking than a child when it is first put to stand against a chair. And when at last I did make a move, it was only to fall forward on my two hands. But I still persevered and, with the aid of chairs and banisters, I was able to visit my room below, which my new housekeeper had just left, her duties being over for the day. To be able to do this, and to prove that I was not so helpless after all, gave me a wonderful feeling of relief and independence. But when Mrs. Larkins, my new housekeeper, came the next morning, I did not tell her anything of what I had done; for I was soon to give her a greater surprise than that, as will be seen in the following chapter.

The next thing I heard of my late housekeeper was that she was out of danger, but owing to having undergone two serious operations, she would not be fit for work for several months. But as she was not coming back to me, I was only sorry about her, and not about myself. For I must now make a confession — I had been a lover now for over three months, and my marriage was only kept waiting on my health.

14: THE END

Here with my treasured Three I sit,
　　Here in my little house of joy,
Sharing one fire, and on one mat:
　　My wife and my dog, Beauty Boy,
And my black Venus of a cat.

But while they sleep I sit and think:
　　Will Death take my black Venus first;
Shall I be first, or Beauty Boy,
　　Or Dinah, whom I love the most —
To leave this little house of joy?

*

It did not take me long to see that Mrs. Larkins was a dishonest woman; that, although I gave her the best price to pay in the market, she did not return with the best things. She also brought in large quantities of food, the sight of which almost destroyed what little appetite I had left; while I, as a weak invalid, could do no more than sip a little hot milk, like a bird at a fountain. However, I was an easy-going fellow, and only once did I offer any complaint. On that occasion I was trying, without much success, to get some lather from a piece of soap that was as hard as a stone, and said at last — 'Mrs. Larkins, why don't you

209　　　　　　　o

buy soap that can be used, even though it cost a guinea an ounce!'

'There's nothing at all the matter with the soap,' answered Mrs. Larkins in a calm voice, 'it's the way you use it.'

When I heard this I began to wonder if there was a great art in using soap, which I, after fifty years of life, had failed to learn, although little children that were not much more than babies could master it at the first attempt.

Under these circumstances it had a wonderful effect on my mind when my strong constitution at last got the mastery over my illness, and I was able to do things for myself. My strength increased day by day; and although the moon might look through my window at night and see me in bed, I would never again give that chance to the midday sun.

So, one fine morning, when Mrs. Larkins came for her daily duties, she not only found me sitting at the table waiting for breakfast, instead of having it in bed, but also dressed and ready to go out. It was quite clear at once that she did not approve of this sudden change, which reminded her of the end of her service. And when I told her I was going out for a walk, and felt strong enough, she sat down for support and, not knowing how to conceal her disappointment, began to abuse a certain teetotal doctor who had not treated her with much civility, all because she had had a small drop of gin and water. 'I went to consult him as a doctor about my poor gums,' said Mrs. Larkins bitterly, 'and did not expect to meet a moral crank and a teetotal maniac.'

I had never seen the poor woman in this strange mood before, and was glad to get away for a time. It was probably this unpleasant change in Mrs. Larkins that made me walk the first hundred yards with more ease than I had expected, for, in thinking of her, I thought less of my own doings.

This was my first walk since my illness, and I managed to reach Hyde Park, which was a mile away. But when I got there I became very much alarmed, owing to being exhausted with my efforts. I was like a swimmer whose eagerness has taken him too far, and made him forget that he has to swim the same distance back, and with less strength too. However, I had the satisfaction of getting back home without any other help than my own.

But it was when I had returned home that the most serious trouble began. For I had to put up with so much annoyance that I was very glad when Mrs. Larkins' duties were over for the day, and I was left alone in peace. For instance, when I lay on my bed helpless and without power to move, my fire often went out for the sake of a little poking while Mrs. Larkins was in the room below. But now, when I was able to look after the fire myself, the wretched woman had the poker in her hand all the time. She poked and she poked, and so viciously that my next-door neighbour, who had always been very quiet, poked back for spite; and the both of them battled with pokers, trying to get at each other, until the noise was terrible.

'Please don't trouble about the fire, Mrs. Larkins,' I said quietly, 'for I am now able to do that myself.'

But these simple words only roused her to more fury, for she made another fierce attack and, of course, my neighbour at once accepted the new challenge, and returned to the battle with all her might. And when Mrs. Larkins was tired at last, and I was glad to get a little peace, she had not been two minutes in her room below before she came rushing up the stairs, shrieking almost hysterically – 'Did you call; what can I do for you – do you want anything?'

It had been her rule, as soon as she had served my midday meal and had her own, to sit at her fire in the room below and take an afternoon nap. She was always in a good condition to do this, for she never forgot to charge me for a large, strong drink to be taken with her meal in the middle of the day. But now, instead of sleeping quietly in the afternoon, she kept on, every quarter of an hour, shrieking from the bottom of the stairs – Did you call?'

How I would have liked to have said – 'Mrs. Larkins, when I *did* call you seldom heard me; and when I wanted anything I often had to ask for it more than once.'

In my weak condition this woman's terrible voice sometimes caught me unawares, especially if I was resting myself and half asleep. Sometimes I thought it was a cry of 'House on fire'; at other times I thought the Great War was still going on, and that I was warned by a former housekeeper, when she had burst into my room with the startled cry of 'The birds are here'; and, looking out of my window, saw a number of the enemy's aeroplanes, in broad daylight too.

However, that I have survived to write these chapters proves that this state of things did not last very long. I do not like calling people by objectionable names, but I must admit that I once called Mrs. Larkins 'Old Raspberry Face' – not in her hearing, of course. For of all the women that ever broke bread or breathed the breath of life, Mrs. Larkins was one of the most unique and original. And to watch the working of that woman's mind, as seen in her face, would be almost as wonderful as to see the fattest lady on earth lifting the smallest man in the world, when he tries to kiss her beneath the mistletoe.

I will now come to the greatest and happiest change in my life: a much greater and happier change than waking one morning in a common lodging-house and finding myself the new and latest poet and the talk of London. This great change had come in my meeting with Helen Payne, whom I now call 'Dinah.' To the world we are William and Helen Davies, but to ourselves we are 'Bunny' and 'Dinah.' How we met and where does not matter; let it be sufficient to say that we came together with as much ease as two drops of rain on a leaf when the wind shakes it.

Young Dinah, whom I had met a few months before my illness, came to see me as often as she could; and we agreed to get married and live in a small country town, leaving London to the care of Mrs. Larkins.

This is what I had been waiting for, and the next thing was to settle down as a married man, somewhere in the green country. I had seen enough of young Dinah to know that she would make a good wife, and it was only a question of whether she had the same confidence in me. She did not like drink and, although I was a drinking man, I was very pleased to see that. For I did not expect any woman to have the same control as a man in the matter of taking drugs. And if it came to having the care of children, when a tin mother would be of more value than a silver father — what would happen if she drank and neglected her home? For there is nothing stronger in the whole world than a mother's example. The effect of drink on men is strangely different; it makes devils of some men and angels of others. But the effect of drink on women is to make devils of them all.

The thought of living with young Dinah in the green country, far from London, had been my one passion during my illness. All my thoughts were set on that great change. One day I was thinking of green leaves, and woods with their own heaven of bluebells; and pools, where I might see the kingfisher dive and brighten his jewels with water. And what dreams I had of passing more trees than human beings and hearing more birds than human voices. Even the night before I had seen in my dreams a tree heavy with red cherries and flaming in a garden. As I looked every cherry turned into a small, red bird, with leaves for wings. And the next moment all those little red birds flew up like one, and away; higher and higher went their little crimson cloud, like Elisha's of old, when he ascended into Heaven in a chariot of fire.

It was not long after this before young Dinah and I were married and settled in a small town in Sussex, about thirty miles from London; where we are now, leading a detached life in a semi-detached house. We have, of course, been subjected to the usual gossip of a small town, but we have not troubled ourselves much about that.

> This little town's a purer place
>   Than any city, rich or poor:
> Six thousand slanderous tongues, that's all –
>   While London has seven millions more.

The one thing that annoyed me, when we first came to live in this little town, was that several people sent in their bills the second time, after having been paid once. When this had happened for the fourth time, I said to my wife – 'Is this a general custom all throughout Sussex, or is it only peculiar to this one little town?'

My wife, who is herself a Sussex girl, answered uncomfortably – 'I don't know what to think of it; but it is not the custom in other parts of Sussex – I am sure of that.'

However, I seldom stay more than five years in one place, and sometimes much less, after which I like a change of people and scenery. And when that time comes I always behave in a strange and a peculiar manner, and do a most unusual thing in paying all my bills and going

away without owing a penny. Some people will
think I am mad, I know, when they hear this;
for even the most honest of people wait for their
bills to follow them, on the chance that trades-
men will not be able to find out their new address,
or think that very small bills are not worth sending at all.

But when I leave I shall be able to say two
good things of Sussex: one is that the beauty
of its countryside nursed me back to good health
and revived my love of Nature; and the other is
that Sussex has given me an excellent little wife.

There is something very primitive about this
little town, in spite of it being so near London.
Sometimes at midnight, or in the early hours of
the morning, people are suddenly roused from
their sleep by a shrill whistle, followed soon after
by two rockets – two terrific bangs, with a long
interval between, which wakes everyone within
a radius of two miles, and sets all the babies crying
and the dogs barking. This means that there is
a fire, generally a hayrick or a barn; but in two
cases out of three it is a false alarm. All this
heavy and tremendous attack on the silent air
is meant to call out the fire brigade, which con-

sists, I believe, of three men. But why these three men cannot be called up for duty in a more gentle way, without disturbing the slumbers of more than six thousand people, not to mention hundreds of babies and dogs — why this cannot be done is not only a mystery to strangers, but is also a mystery to most of the natives.

In spite of saying these things against this little town, I must admit that the police are very nice indeed; for if I venture down the main street, they always turn their heads, so as to give me a chance to get away.

But although I may leave this part of the world at any time, after I have become too familiar with the beauty of my surroundings, I have not the least intention of returning to London, or any other large town or city. There appears to be no end to my liking for Nature; whether a tree is so leafy that it reduces the whole heavens to a few blue eyes, or whether the twigs are as thin and bare as the birds' legs that use them — it is all the same to me.

We were soon busy planting here and there in the garden; so that the following summer should have such a blaze of colour that I hoped to have as my guests not only hundreds of bees and butterflies, but also the great dragonfly, with his crowned head, and his breast covered with shining honours. As for young Dinah, she had a green hand; for every brown seed she planted in the earth grew and came to leaf, and reached the age of blossom – for nothing seemed to die.

At the present time, while I am writing this, we have just left Christmas behind, and are at the beginning of a New Year. On Christmas morning the mantelpiece was like a cattle-market, stocked with horses and cows of chocolate, with sheep and fat pigs made of white sugar. Long chains of coloured paper were hanging from the highest corners, which I once thought only a spider or fly could reach. Here and there I saw large gorgeous parasols and fans, with Chinese lanterns too; while from the ceiling hung large balloons, round, oval and sausage-shaped. Everywhere I looked I saw either a quaint little man or woman, or a young cherub; or boxes covered with silver tinsel, which contained – but that was young Dinah's secret, and was only to be known by me at a certain time. It was the most gorgeous room I had ever seen, and yet it was all built up with odd pennies; this cost twopence-half-penny, and that cost a penny more; and two or three things cost a little silver, but nothing cost gold. The effect was rich indeed; and I soon heard that young Dinah had been getting these things together in secret for some time past, so as to give me a Christmas Eve of surprise and wonder.

During this Christmas season young Dinah and I have pulled sixty and eight bonbons, not to mention one huge fellow in particular, that was over two feet long! The sudden report and bangs of these bonbons did not give quite so much pleasure to our dog, Beauty Boy, or our black Venus of a cat, as it did to ourselves. But if they suffered at all, it was more from annoyance than fear.

Our greatest surprises came of course on Christmas morning. For we had both bought each other a number of presents, with so much generosity that we had to use pillow-slips, instead of the usual stockings, to hold them. These pillow-slips, full of presents, were to be taken into the bedroom and, as soon as the light was put out, were to be exchanged in the dark, and not opened until the next morning. All this was done according to plan, except that my wife woke at daybreak and insisted on the pillow-slips being opened at once. Unfortunately, at this very moment our neighbour's cockerel began to crow in such a flat, horrible voice that young Dinah said – 'That poor bird has a severe cold.'

There was certainly something wrong with the bird, for Beauty Boy, who slept outside our bedroom door, barked furiously – a thing he had never done before at that early hour of the morning. As it was impossible to sleep again, under these conditions, we opened our pillow-slips there and then and enjoyed the sight of our presents.

Just as I finish writing this book my little den upstairs, where I do my writing, is invaded by a dog and a cat. These two have now been given their liberty, and the first thing they do with it is to seek their master, to let him know that it is tea-time downstairs. The dog, Beauty Boy, struts around, with his long tail beating the drum against the various objects in the room. But the black Venus of a cat sits, without any demonstration, on the head of my couch, staring at me with her large eyes. When I played with her this morning her eyes were all yellow, except two pupils that were no more than two thin lines like the strokes of a pen. But when I look at her now, the pupils are large, round, black balls, and the yellow circles are as thin as an old woman's ring.

When I am ready for tea, Beauty Boy rushes off in advance, to let my wife, young Dinah, know that I am on the way. But the Black Venus sits motionless: *She* has only come up to see me on one condition, that I *carry* her down.